FORAGING MUSHROOMS MAINE

Help Us Keep This Guide Up to Date

Every effort has been made by the author and editors to make this guide as accurate and useful as possible. However, many things can change after a guide is published.

    We would appreciate hearing from you concerning your experiences with this guide and how you feel it could be improved and kept up to date. While we may not be able to respond to all comments and suggestions, we'll take them to heart, and we'll also make certain to share them with the authors. Please send your comments and suggestions to the following address:

FalconGuides
Reader Response/Editorial Department
246 Goose Lane
Guilford, CT 06437

Or you may e-mail us at: editorial@falcon.com

Thanks for your input, and happy foraging!

FORAGING MUSHROOMS MAINE

Finding, Identifying, and Preparing Edible Wild Mushrooms

Tom Seymour

FALCONGUIDES

GUILFORD, CONNECTICUT

An imprint of Globe Pequot

Falcon and FalconGuides are registered trademarks and Make Adventure Your Story is a trademark of Rowman & Littlefield.

Distributed by NATIONAL BOOK NETWORK

Photos by Tom Seymour unless otherwise noted
Text contributions by Jim Meuninck for King Bolete and Crown Coral
Map: Melissa Baker © Rowman & Littlefield

Printed in the United States of America

British Library Cataloguing-in-Publication Information available

Library of Congress Cataloging-in-Publication Data

Names: Seymour, Tom, author.
Title: Foraging mushrooms Maine : finding, identifying, and preparing edible wild mushrooms /
 Tom Seymour.
Description: Guilford, Connecticut : FalconGuides, 2017. | Includes index. |
  Identifiers: LCCN 2017004991 (print) | LCCN 2017021282 (ebook) | ISBN 9781493022953 (e-book)
  | ISBN 9781493022946 (pbk. : alk. paper)
Subjects: LCSH: Edible mushrooms—Maine—Identification. | Cooking (Mushrooms)
Classification: LCC QK605.5.M2 (ebook) | LCC QK605.5.M2 S49 2017 (print) |
  DDC 641.3/58--dc23
LC record available at https://lccn.loc.gov/2017004991

♾™ The paper used in this publication meets the minimum requirements of American National Standard for Information Sciences—Permanence of Paper for Printed Library Materials, ANSI/NISO Z39.48-1992.

To the memory of Eleanor Avener, a kind, gentle, soft-spoken naturalist who loved everything nature had to offer.

The identification, selection, and processing of any wild plant, fungus, or mushroom for use as food requires reasonable care and attention to details since, as indicated in the text, certain mushrooms are wholly unsuitable for use and, in some instances, are even toxic. Because attempts to use any wild plants, fungus, or mushrooms for food depend on various factors controllable only by the reader, the author and Globe Pequot assume no liability for personal accident, illness, or death related to these activities.

This book is a work of reference. Readers should always consult an expert before using any foraged item. The authors, editors, and publisher of this work have checked with sources believed to be reliable in their efforts to confirm the accuracy and completeness of the information presented herein and that the information is in accordance with the standard practices accepted at the time of publication. However, neither the authors, editors, and publisher, nor any other party involved in the creation and publication of this work warrant that the information is in every respect accurate and complete, and they are not responsible for errors or omissions or for any consequences from the application of the information in this book. In light of ongoing research and changes in clinical experience and in governmental regulations, readers are encouraged to confirm the information contained herein with additional sources. This book does not purport to be a complete presentation of all plants, fungus, or mushrooms, and the genera, species, and cultivars discussed or pictured herein are but a small fraction of the plants, fungus, or mushrooms found in the wild, in an urban or suburban landscape, or in a home. Given the global movement of plants, fungus, and mushrooms, we would expect continual introduction of species having toxic properties to the regions discussed in this book. We have made every attempt to be botanically and mycologically accurate, but regional variations in plant, fungus, and mushroom names, growing conditions, and availability may affect the accuracy of the information provided. A positive identification of an individual plant, fungus, or mushroom is most likely when a freshly collected part of the plant containing leaves and flowers or fruits, or a mushroom including the base is presented to a knowledgeable botanist, mycologist, or horticulturist, depending on what you're foraging. Poison Control Centers generally have relationships with the botanical and mycological community should the need for plant, fungus, or mushroom identification arises. We have attempted to provide accurate descriptions of plants, fungus, or mushrooms, but there is no substitute for direct interaction with a trained botanist, horticulturist, or mycologist for proper identification. **In cases of exposure or ingestion, contact a Poison Control Center (800-222-1222), a medical toxicologist, another appropriate health-care provider, or an appropriate reference resource.**

CONTENTS

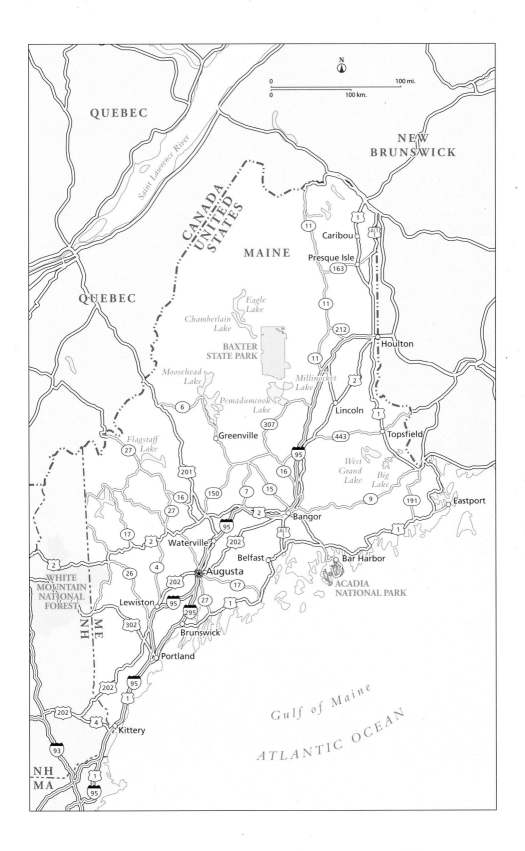

INTRODUCTION

Mushrooms of Maine

My fondness for wild mushrooms goes back to early childhood when, as I was visiting a friend, wild mushrooms were on the menu. My pal's parents called my parents to secure permission to serve me wild mushrooms and permission was granted.

The mushrooms were small puffballs, cut in half and fried to a golden brown. This initial introduction got me "hooked" on wild mushrooms. All the same, it was not until my teen years that I dared to search for wild mushrooms on my own. And at that, my list of known safe mushrooms was quite short. Fear of making a deadly mistake kept me from having a cavalier attitude toward mushroom identification.

My approach to wild mushrooms has never changed. And that is to get to know one mushroom inside and out before going on to another species. One at a time, slow but steady, learn the texture, the scent: know the spore print color; and determine if there are any toxic look-alikes. Get to know each mushroom so well that not the slightest chance of error exists. And then, after assimilating all information and data regarding one single mushroom, it is safe to go about finding and learning another.

It is virtually impossible to be too careful when dealing with wild mushrooms. Those new to the hobby should adopt this attitude. That way, when it comes time to sit down and sample a new mushroom, there will be no lingering doubt to cloud the experience.

Mushroom Mindset

Different people have differing thoughts regarding wild mushrooms. To some, mushrooms are a source of seasonal income. More and more people range out through woods and meadows in search of salable mushrooms. The emergence of "natural" restaurants, those featuring locally grown as well as wild-harvested produce, have bred the new, profit-seeking mushroom hunter. To these people, wild mushrooms always come with a dollar sign.

Others, such as the author, view wild mushrooms in a whole different light. Rather than simply being a product to be exploited, wild mushrooms are part and parcel of the larger bounty offered by nature. And as such, we who truly appreciate the wild offerings available to us would freely give of our harvest but would never, ever sell it.

Some people devote much effort and energy to learning about mushrooms. Professional mycologists spend little time on anything else, mushroom seeking, harvesting, and teaching being their one focus. Others, such as the author, are foragers first and amateur mycologists second.

In the author's case, it has taken many years to learn about and become comfortable with the mushrooms currently in his purview. This probably has as much to do with the capricious nature of mushrooms as anything else. Some mushrooms just don't appear in large numbers but rather show up one here, one there. And sometimes mushrooms do not reappear in the places where they were found the previous year.

It is impractical to expect to simply walk in the woods in late summer or early fall and harvest edible mushrooms. Mushrooms are where you find them, and there's little we can do to change that. Certainly we can expect to find some mushrooms during our woodland walks, but so often these are of an unknown variety or, when of a known type, are toxic. People used to call toxic mushrooms "toadstools." Really though, they are all mushrooms. It's just that some are edible and some are not.

Familiar Friends

Once someone new to wild mushrooms becomes totally familiar with two or three varieties, something special happens. The mushrooms become like old friends. Typically (though, as pointed out earlier, not always), mushrooms tend to appear in the same places year after year. That's because the area satisfies their needs. And yes, all mushrooms, like all plants, have very specific needs. Some require an acidic setting such as is found in pine groves. Others need direct sunlight, and some thrive in the dappled light of mixed-growth woods.

Much of the author's mushroom hunting takes place from the driver's seat of his car. Several wild mushrooms are so stylized and distinct that they can be spotted from afar, even at highway speeds (which in rural Maine is typically 45 miles per hour). Here's a for instance.

While returning home one September day, an orange blur, partway up a dying cherry tree, caught the author's eye. After stopping and backing up for a better look, it was plain that the tree hosted a great number of chicken of the woods, *Laetiporus sulphureus*, shelf-type mushrooms. Their orange color, plus their habit of growing often great distances up a tree, was a sure giveaway. No other mushrooms look quite like *L. sulphureus*, so it was a good bet that even when first spotted from the car, that these were chicken of the woods mushrooms.

Likewise, several roadsides near the author's home host large puffball mushrooms. These appear virtually overnight in September and into October. Growing on the gravel strip on soft shoulders of rural roads, these mushrooms are easy to spot, even from a moving vehicle. These big puffballs, *Calvatia* species, are usually the only kind of mushrooms to grow in this admittedly hostile environment.

Being so keen on picking roadside puffballs, the author has more than once stopped for a mushroom that turned out to be nothing more than a discarded paper cup. From a distance, white cups and white mushrooms look very similar.

Another familiar mushroom, the meadow mushroom, *Agaricus campestris*, typically appears on lawns and other grassy areas where the grass doesn't get too high. These, too, are easily spotted while driving along. Looking very much like the cap-style mushrooms sold in supermarkets, these are rated "choice" by most collectors. Distinctions such as this are of course a matter of taste and taste is subjective. Nevertheless, a choice listing means that most people will find the mushroom tasty.

Meadow mushrooms have a few decidedly unfriendly look-alikes, and the way to tell the difference between a delicious, safe meadow mushroom and a toxic look-alike is described in detail in the chapter on meadow mushrooms and also here in the introduction in the Identification section. But for now, suffice it to say that meadow mushrooms, when present, are easily spotted.

Note that many times, meadow mushrooms will appear on private property. The author has never been denied permission, after asking, to stop and harvest mushrooms. It's a safe bet that if the landowner knew or cared about wild mushrooms, they would already have been harvested.

Sometimes, though, meadow mushrooms appear in public places such as school lawns or town hall lawns. Most of the time, these are fair game.

Regular Mushroom Spots
Some mushrooms come up each year in the same place. There are exceptions and it is impossible to predict whether or not mushrooms will appear in the same area in any given year. But often as not, once located, many mushrooms can be counted on to come up in the same location, year after year.

Having ascertained a number of mushroom-producing locations, it's a good plan to keep records of when the mushrooms were harvested. Usually, a mushroom species will appear at close to the same time each year. There are exceptions such as years with prolonged droughts or wet spells. These can alter the emergence dates of wild mushrooms.

But here again, we can deal only with the situation at hand, and if we have kept a log of where and when we harvested any particular species of mushroom, we can presume to have a slight advantage concerning finding the mushrooms again each year.

This is the case with the author's woodlot. Several species of mushrooms make regular, annual appearances. Some years there are more and some years there are fewer. And some years, not a single mushroom will appear where the year before there were hundreds. Anyone who owns or has permission to go mushroom hunting on a woodlot or other property can pretty much predict when and what kind of mushrooms will appear there year after year. That's the beauty of having regular mushroom spots.

Finding new mushroom locations requires both luck and diligence. Never write off a place that should have mushrooms but had none at the time of your visit. Subsequent visits may prove fruitful. On the other hand, some excellent mushroom locations are found purely by accident. Consider these the low-hanging fruit and be grateful for them. Good mushroom locations are something to be cherished.

Can Mushrooms Sustain Harvesting?

A participant at one of the author's wild plant seminars once asked if picking too many mushrooms from one place could harm the resource. "Is it sustainable?" he asked. Here is the answer he got. It's an analogy, but a fitting one. Consider mushrooms as something similar to apples on a tree. It doesn't hurt to pick all the apples from a tree because they would eventually drop off on their own or be eaten by animals. The tree has no idea what happens to its fruit. An apple tree's only duty is to set fruits and bring them to maturity.

It's the same with mushrooms. The fruiting body, the actual fleshy part of the fungi, grows above ground, and the mycelium, or spawn, which is something like a mass of slender threads, lives and feeds beneath the ground. In nature, the above-ground part, what we call the "mushroom," drops countless, minute spores. These ride on the air currents and can find themselves distributed a considerable distance from the mushroom. The spores germinate upon landing on the ground. After germinating, the spores form more spawn, which, in turn, will send up more above-ground fruiting bodies.

So while it won't hurt to pick all of the mushrooms around, it also helps to leave a few so that they can propagate and make more mushrooms. But even in areas that have been heavily picked, a few late-arriving mushrooms usually materialize to keep the process going.

Identification

The possibility of harvesting and later ingesting a toxic species dictates that foragers make 100 percent accurate identifications. Mushrooms, like other plants, have certain qualities that aid in identification. When and if just one feature of any particular mushroom does not agree with those mentioned in a guidebook, then the mushroom is not the species in question.

For instance, if the forager finds a cap-style mushroom growing on a lawn, it is not enough to simply match the mushroom to the photograph in a book. Certainly, that is an important part of the identification process, but it is only the first step in a many-parted procedure.

Let us imagine that the mushroom on the lawn is thought to be a meadow mushroom (also called pink bottom), *Agaricus campestris*. The book says that this mushroom has a flat or sometimes convex cap, 1½ to 4 inches wide. The cap is white or whitish, in mature specimens tending toward various shades of brown, dry to the touch, smooth, and, in some cases, scaly.

The gills in the button (immature stage, not yet umbrella-shaped, but more like a puffball, since the cap has not yet expanded) stage are white, turning pink as the mushroom matures (thus the common name) and becoming brown to blackish with age. The gills are free from the stem, meaning that they don't quite touch the stem. There is a little open space between gills and stem, kind of like a moat. The cap, once the mushroom assumes its "umbrella" form (just like the common mushrooms sold in the supermarket), exhibits a ragged fringe on its edge. This is the remnant of the "veil" that united cap and stem in the button stage. As the umbrella unfolded it tore the veil, leaving noticeable fringing. Also, the rest of the veil, or *annulus*, hangs like a ring around the stem. The stem grows up to 3 inches long, is cylinder-shaped and white throughout. Meadow mushrooms leave a chocolate-brown spore print.

Any deviation from these attributes marks the mushroom at hand as a possibly toxic species. Also, any physical feature other than that noted in the book is also a warning that this may be a toxic mushroom. For instance, beginning foragers may confuse an edible meadow mushroom with the deadly toxic destroying angel, *Amanita virosa*. However, *A. virosa* is a chalky-white mushroom with a ring on the stem, with or without a sac-like cup at the base of the stem. Also, *A. virosa* has a distinct, bleach-like smell, made more conspicuous when the mushroom is cut or broken. Finally, *A. virosa* leaves a white spore print. Always avoid any mushroom with these features. Especially look for the stem cup.

This brings to mind the great importance of harvesting the entire mushroom. Never just break the stem off at ground level. This may leave the underground part of the stem, along with a cup, if present, undetected in the ground. Use the fingers to move earth around the base of the stem so as to remove the mushroom in its entirety.

Spore Prints

Let's assume that careful inspection indicates that the mushroom at hand is indeed a meadow mushroom. The next step, the one that clinches the identification, is to make a spore print. Cap-type mushrooms drop spores, and when the spores drop on a sheet of paper, they show up in various colors. We know now that meadow mushroom, *A. campestris*, leaves a chocolate-brown spore print and destroying angel, *A. virosa*, leaves a white spore print.

Taking spore prints is an interesting pastime in and of itself, since the prints differ in size and color from one mushroom to another. Some prints are so singularly striking that they are worth mounting in a picture frame. But the real value of spore prints is to help us in identifying mushrooms.

Spores in a mushroom are tiny, numbering in the millions. Being so tiny, even the slightest wind or breeze can disrupt the hoped-for pattern when making a spore print. There is a way to circumvent this and that is to put a cup or bowl over the mushroom while making a spore print. This keeps air movement away from the spores.

The way to make a spore print from a cap-style mushroom is as follows. First, remove the stem, being careful to keep the cap intact. Next, in anticipation of what color spore print the mushroom will make, select a sheet of paper that will offer the best contrast between spore print and paper. Gently place the cap, gill-side down, on the paper and place a cup or bowl over the cap.

Time lengths vary for mushrooms to drop all their spores. The author likes to start the procedure in the afternoon and leave the mushroom on the paper, out of the sun and out of wind, until the following morning. Then, lift the cup or bowl, remove the cap and look for the spore print. This looks something like an old-fashioned photographic negative. If all other qualifying features in the book are met and the spore print is the same color as the book says it should be, then the identification is complete. Of course if the spore print is a different color, the mushroom should be discarded.

Experts sometimes go a step further in their identification process, using a microscope to make finite distinctions. This is beyond the scope of this book. The mushroom species contained here are all quite common and not particularly difficult to identify, as long as proper protocol, as set out here, is followed.

For other than cap-style mushrooms, and there are some in this book, the same criteria must be followed in the identification process. Any mushroom not meeting all the qualifying features is considered to be an unknown entity and must not be eaten.

Avoiding Toxic Plants

Going outside seeking useful mushrooms invariably brings the forager near or in contact with some very nasty plants. In Maine, two plants to definitely avoid are poison ivy, *Rhus radicans*, and virgin's bower, *Clematis virginiana*.

Poison ivy, much to the chagrin of unlucky people who have accidentally come in contact with it, has a highly variable form. Sometimes poison ivy presents itself as a trailing or even a climbing vine. And other times it grows as an erect plant, often reaching shrub status. But whatever form the stalk assumes, the leaves are key to proper identification.

Poison ivy leaves always come in groups of three. Instead of the saw-like "teeth" of many other plants, the margin, or leaf edges, have irregular, gentle, sometimes notch-like indentations. These leaves, green with sometimes a trace of red, are always shiny.

Although the leaves are borne in groups of three, the bottom two, opposite each other at the end of the stem, are separated from the top leaf by a small section of stalk. In other words, the three leaves of poison ivy do not all radiate from a common point.

The best way to prevent poison ivy rash is to not allow exposed skin to touch it at all. It helps, then, to wear long pants and long-sleeved shirts when afield. Also, an effective poison ivy remedy, jewelweed, *Impatiens carpensis* (see *Foraging New England*, a FalconGuide, 2002, 2013), usually grows not far from where poison ivy is found. Just break off some jewelweed stems, crush them by hand, and rub the resulting juice on the skin that touched poison ivy. This will circumvent poison ivy rash. A thorough washing with soap and water upon returning home completes the cure.

Virgin's bower, *C. virginiana*, also called wild clematis, is as insidious as poison ivy in that it can grow thickly over trails and paths but blends in with the background so as not to be noticed. The leaves, in groups of three like poison ivy, are wider than poison ivy leaves and may be said to resemble the general shape of leaves of red maple, *Acer rubrum*. Also, unlike poison ivy, virgin's bower leaves have more prominent teeth, often quite sharp. The leaf blade exhibits a strong venation pattern.

Virgin's bower has clusters of small, white flowers borne on long, spindly stalks. Fruit clusters follow the flowers, and these have long, plume-like tails, which accounts for the common name of virgin's bower.

The danger to casual foragers and other walkers in the wild is of encountering virgin's bower vines and not knowing it. If one of these should fall across a person's exposed neck or arms, a long-lasting, uncomfortable rash may develop. So again, prevention outweighs the need to seek a cure. Because of that, always keep an eye out for any kind of vine when in thick cover. If a vine looks even a little bit like virgin's bower, avoid it. And if exposure does occur, follow the same cure procedure as for poison ivy.

Enjoying Mushrooms Safely

Since the possibility of poisoning exists when ingesting an unidentified wild mushroom, never, ever eat or even nibble on any mushroom that you are unsure of. Add to this warning an admonition not to eat wild mushrooms raw. Unlike supermarket mushrooms, which many people enjoy raw and sliced on salads, wild mushrooms can present unpleasant consequences if eaten raw.

For instance, hen of the woods, *Grifola frondosa*, a delicious mushroom when cut up in small bits and fried in butter, has a harsh, bitter taste if eaten raw and can cause gastrointestinal distress. Other mushrooms hold similarly unpleasant surprises.

So again, to avoid unpleasant (or worse) consequences, never eat any wild mushroom raw and never eat any wild mushroom if you are at all unsure about its identification.

Also, even upon identifying a fine, edible mushroom, it is best to eat just a tiny bit at first. Cut up a small portion of mushroom and fry it, and then eat just a small amount. Save the uncooked remainder in a cool spot and cover in case further identification is needed. Then, if no unpleasant symptoms develop, it's okay to eat a larger quantity the next day.

Some mushrooms, even perfectly safe ones, sometimes don't agree with certain individuals. In other words, not everyone can eat any particular edible mushroom with no side effects. So for that reason it is best to try just a teeny bit first.

Note also that some otherwise fine, edible mushrooms don't go well with alcohol because they react to it in a person's system. If a drinker, then either avoid these mushrooms or do not have them while consuming alcohol.

Mushroom Myths

A friend once asked me to explain the difference between mushrooms and toadstools. I told him that they were both one and the same. His perplexed look prompted me to further explain the genesis of mushrooms and toadstools.

In years past, all poisonous mushrooms were generically lumped into the broad group known as "toadstools." But this led to confusion and people had a difficult time because the word "toadstool" suggested a distinct and separate genus. But in fact, there is no difference. All are mushrooms. Thankfully, toadstools have been pretty much deleted from the mushroom hunter's lexicon.

What was even worse in the old days were the various methods of determining whether or not a specimen was a mushroom or a toadstool. One utterly false concept was that if animals can eat a mushroom (or toadstool) with impunity, then it was safe for humans. The truth is that animals have no inherent ability to discern between safe and poisonous mushrooms. Here's an example of this.

One day a friend of the author's asked if a certain mushroom on his lawn was safe to eat. We walked out and there it was, an *A. virosa*, or destroying angel. The mushroom was definitely toxic and in fact, belonged to a wider group of the world's deadliest mushrooms.

As it happened, some critter had taken an obvious bite from the mushroom's cap. And not far from that lay a dead mouse. Pointing first at the mushroom and then at the dead rodent, the author asked his friend, "Well, what do you think?" That was enough to instill a profound respect for the power of poison mushrooms in the author's friend.

In truth, the dead mouse was probably not the animal that had nibbled on the toxic mushroom. But its proximity to the partly eaten, toxic mushroom provided a meaningful and profound teachable moment.

Another age-old bit of foolish folklore states that a poison mushroom will turn silverware dark if inserted in the flesh, but if the same knife or fork was inserted into an edible mushroom, it would remain shiny. Even a hundred years ago many people must have thought that such a test was simply rubbish.

The reality is that there are no hard-and-fast rules for determining whether a mushroom is edible or toxic. The only way to know is to study each mushroom individually, comparing every word of the description in a field guide to the specimen in hand and then making a spore print for further confirmation. It's not as romantic as just saying a mushroom is a toadstool, but it's an awful lot safer.

Look-Alikes

Some fine, edible wild mushrooms have toxic look-alikes. The way to tell the difference between a perfectly safe mushroom and a toxic look-alike is to follow all the steps outlined in the section on identification. No matter how closely a safe mushroom may resemble a toxic mushroom, there are always certain characteristics that separate the safe from the toxic.

So always follow each step in proper identification and you will never mistake a safe mushroom for a toxic one.

Legal Considerations

Commercial harvesting of mushrooms is a hot topic lately. A bill that would mandate commercial harvesters and recreational harvesters secure landowner permission is being considered by Maine lawmakers.

Both commercial and amateur mushroom hunters are strongly encouraged to seek landowner permission when harvesting on private lands, since landowners who feel a resource is being wrongly removed from their property can simply post "No Trespassing" signs, preventing all access. In Maine, while fish and game are a public resource and not the personal property of any landowner, mushrooms and wild plants in general are the property of the landowner. Therefore, harvesting without permission is considered theft.

Regarding public lands, managing agencies may allow harvesting of mushrooms and wild plants. Others may prohibit any harvesting at all. Always check with the managing entity before harvesting any mushroom or wild product from any public lands.

As mentioned earlier, the author has never been denied the opportunity to pick mushrooms on private property. So just ask. Chances are the landowner will appreciate being asked and will extend permission to harvest.

And when asking permission, make certain to point out that you are an individual collector picking wild mushrooms for personal use and not a commercial harvester. Explain that you have no intention of selling any wild mushrooms. Often, private landowners will deny permission to commercial harvesters but allow individual mushroom hunters to explore and pick whatever they may find.

Finally, if receiving permission to collect wild mushrooms on private property, it is always a nice gesture to offer the landowner some of your harvest, while explaining how to safely prepare it. This goes a long way toward establishing a long-term relationship.

Endangered Species

Maine has no endangered mushroom, although one plant on the Maine endangered list, autumn coralroot, lacks the green pigment typical of most flowering plants. But being a flowering plant, autumn coralroot is not a fungus.

Tools and Techniques

Harvesting mushrooms does not require a lot of specialized equipment. Most everyone has the tools needed to harvest wild mushrooms. Some backyard mushroom hunters go afield armed with only a basket. A basket is preferable to a plastic bag or other nonrigid container because it helps keep the mushrooms from being crushed and it allows for air circulation so the mushrooms don't become soft or mushy.

However, it is always good to have some means of segregating mushrooms in the basket. Sometimes a forager will find both known and unknown varieties. If stored together in a basket, the unknown mushrooms may become mixed in with known ones. And if the unknown variety turns out to be toxic, problems could result.

So do keep different varieties separate when placing in basket or canvas bag. The best way to do this is to wrap each different kind of mushroom in waxed paper. This will keep them from spoiling, while segregating unknown varieties for safety's sake. The known varieties of mushrooms can be stored without being segregated.

Certain mushroom varieties such as shelf-type mushrooms grow on trees, and a knife, even a jackknife, makes harvesting easier. A knife (ideally an old knife, one that won't suffer from hard use) also facilitates digging the entire stalk of cap-type mushrooms in hard soil. Digging at the base of the stem with a knife helps to ascertain if there is a cup, or bulblike end to the stem, perhaps signaling that the mushroom is a toxic *Amanita* species.

Finally, a mushroom guide such as this one can come in handy when afield.

Preparation and Storage Tips

To prepare mushrooms for storage or immediate cooking requires thoroughly cleaning all debris and clinging material from the mushrooms. Never clean a mushroom wet, because this drives foreign matter in the gills, making it almost impossible to remove.

So, then, mushrooms must always be cleaned when perfectly dry. Sometimes this is just a matter of removing a few bits of moss or twigs by hand. But when cleaning gill-type mushrooms it is often necessary to dig into the gills and for this, the author recommends a jackknife with a long, slender point. Toothpicks work, too. Some people sacrifice a new toothbrush for scrubbing foreign matter out of mushroom gills.

Mushrooms keep several days or even longer when stored in the crisper drawer of a refrigerator. But storing the mushrooms uncovered can lead to them becoming dried out and essentially worthless. So keep mushrooms in a plastic bag, loosely closed, and they will keep in good shape until they are used.

Most amateur mushroom enthusiasts eat most of the mushrooms they gather when fresh. But a bumper crop can stifle even the most enthusiastic mushroom fan. In that case, it makes sense to preserve the mushrooms somehow. There are three ways to do this. These are freezing, drying and pressure canning.

Freezing ranks as the most popular form of mushroom preservation. Frozen mushrooms look, taste and feel much like the fresh product. To freeze any mushroom, cut it into fairly small bits and slowly fry in your favorite spread. Clarified butter works well for this because it won't easily burn, but many people don't care to go to the trouble of clarifying butter. Oil works too, but it can make the mushrooms, well, oily. Oil doesn't come very highly recommended. The author has had best results using a buttery spread made with olive oil. In this case, the mushrooms absorb much of the spread and there is no oily residue.

Certain mushrooms lend themselves to drying. A home dehydrator makes quick work of a basket of mushrooms. For this, the mushrooms must be sliced thin so that they can dry evenly. After drying for the recommended time, the mushrooms can be stored in an airtight container and will keep for a year and perhaps more.

A simpler drying method works well for those who have woodstoves in their home. First slice the mushrooms thin and then, using a large needle, thread all the mushroom slices on a string. When the mushroom "garland" is complete, tack both ends of the string to the mantle or wall in a way that heat from the stove will expedite drying. Don't have the strung mushrooms to close to the stove, or else they will cook before they dry.

Only a very few people put their mushrooms up by home pressure canning. In fact, the home-canner's "bible," *Ball Blue Book*, states that mushrooms are better frozen than canned. However, the guidebook that came with the author's Mirro-brand home canner includes a recipe for mushrooms.

The procedure for home-canning mushrooms, according to Mirro, is to trim the mushrooms and then soak them in cold water for 10 minutes. Large mushrooms should be cut in half. Cook gently for 15 minutes (this can be by simmering in water), drain and pack hot in jars. Cover with boiling water, leaving a half-inch headspace. Pressure-cook pints and half-pints for 45 minutes at 10 pounds of pressure.

The author has used this recipe for pressure-canning small puffball mushrooms. The mushrooms were cut in half before processing. The result was similar in texture, and even taste, to store-bought canned mushrooms. These mushrooms lasted for several years with no appreciable diminishing of quality.

Reasons for Foraging

So why forage anyway? Perfectly fine mushrooms are available in most stores, and it's a lot easier to just pick a package or two off the shelf than to walk through woods and fields, looking for wild mushrooms. Besides, mushrooms are mushrooms, aren't they?

All the above is certainly true. But lately, more and more people are discovering the advantages of acquiring their own food rather than relying upon commercial enterprises to supply it for them.

It's sort of like the idea that milk doesn't really come from a container in the store's cooler but rather, it comes from a cow. And so on. Our society has become disassociated from the real world, the world that has biting insects and dangerous plants but also gives us delicious morsels of wild foods, including mushrooms, that treat our palate and contribute to our good health.

And this doesn't even address the immense satisfaction that comes from finding, identifying, harvesting, preparing, and finally eating your own foraged foods. There's more, too. Foragers, even beginning ones who know just a few mushrooms (or edible wild plants), experience at least to a small degree a feeling of independence.

Besides all this, foraging is just plain practical. Wild foods come to us straight from the woods and fields. They aren't treated with pesticides and they aren't hybridized to extend their shelf life. Because of this, they have full flavor, flavors that those who forage only in supermarket shelves have never tasted.

And speaking of practicality, many of us have mushrooms and wild edible plants growing on our property. Most of the time, these are far more healthful than the food we buy. Does it really make sense to buy spinach when dandelions are ready for picking? Likewise, it is impractical to drive to the store to buy button mushrooms when delicious, wild meadow mushrooms are growing on our lawn.

So for foragers, it's really a combination of the practical and the aesthetic that fuels our efforts. Be forewarned, though. Once a forager, always a forager. It's easy to learn how to forage, but almost impossible to quit once you start out. Foraging, then, is a life skill, one that will serve you well anywhere and anytime.

Mushroom State of Mind

So many things we do in life are a result of ingrained responses. In the case of hunting for wild mushrooms, the quest never ends, and for some, it has no real beginnings, because during the season, seasoned mushroom foragers always have one eye open for useful, wild mushrooms. In other words, we develop a "mushroom state of mind."

In the author's case, a collecting basket and canvas collecting bag are never far away. So when I'm hiking, hunting, fishing, or leading field trips for wild edibles, mushrooms are always a possibility. Once, lacking anything else, the author filled the game pocket of his upland hunting coat with oyster mushrooms.

In another instance, a spare jacket served to hold hundreds of small puffballs gathered from an exposed slope. All of this points to having a mushroom state of mind. So when the opportunity presents itself, and it surely will, take advantage of a new find and pick those wild mushrooms when and where they are encountered.

Scope of this Guide

Bookshelves abound with mushroom guides directed to those who want to jump headfirst into the hobby. Some people, though, would like to begin with a simple guidebook, something that doesn't detail too many species of mushrooms so as to become confusing. These folks want a book that shows them a good spectrum of the common, edible wild mushrooms in Maine.

So for those who have toyed with the idea of checking to see if those mushrooms on the back lawn, or those shelf-type mushrooms growing on an ancient white ash tree are edible, this is the book for you.

My thoughts on doing this book were that it would be difficult for me, a forager in general and not necessarily a mushroom specialist, to add anything to the bulk of knowledge that already exists. But my Globe Pequot editor David Legere convinced me otherwise. Dave said that this book would be aimed at beginners, homeowners, and others who would like to learn a little more about the mushrooms around them.

So with that thought in mind, Globe Pequot and I offer this book, a book whose goal is to help people who would like to learn a little bit more about the mushrooms around them.

SPECIES LIST

Gem-Studded Puffball, *Lycoperdon perlatum*

Giant Puffball, *Calvatia gigantea*

Pear-Shaped Puffball, *Lycoperdon pyriforme*

Fairy Ring, *Marasmius oreades*

Meadow Mushroom, Pink Bottom, *Agaricus campestris*

Mica Cap, *Coprinus micaceus*

Oyster Mushroom, *Pleurotus ostreatus*

Shaggy Mane, Lawyer's Wig, *Coprinus comatus*

Yellow Waxy Cap, *Hygrocybe flavescens*

Artist's Conk, *Ganoderma applanatum*

Chaga, *Inonotus obliquus*

Chicken of the Woods, Sulphur Shelf, *Laetiporus sulphureus*

Hen of the Woods, *Grifola frondosa*

Turkey Tail, *Trametes versicolor*

Black Trumpet, Death Trumpet, Horn of Plenty, *Craterellus fallax*

Chanterelle, *Cantharellus cibarius*

Red Chanterelle, *Cantharellus cinnabarinus*

King Bolete, *Boletaceae*

Painted Bolete, *Suillus spraguei*, also sometimes referred to as *Suillus pictus*

Red-Cracked Bolete, *Boletus chrysenteron*

Bear's Head Tooth, *Hericium coralloides*

Spreading Hydnum, *Hydnum repandum*

Crown Coral, *Artomyces pyxidata*

Lobster, *Hypomyces lactifluorum*

1   Puffballs

GEM-STUDDED PUFFBALL
Lycoperdon perlatum

Identification: Height about 2 inches, pear-shaped with spines, or "gems," that are easily rubbed off with the fingers. Older specimens have vent, or orifice, in middle of top. When the mushroom matures and produces spores, the slightest touch makes the spores "puff" out of the vent, thus the common name. When sliced in half, flesh is firm and pure white.

Habitat: On soil, edges of lawns, gravel areas, in mixed-growth woodlands, and even on compost.

Use: Cooked.

Range: Throughout Maine, a truly cosmopolitan mushroom.

Similarity to toxic species: Because of the spines the mushroom should not be confused with any toxic species. If in doubt, slice in half longitudinally, and if the flesh is pure white and there is no cap-style mushroom image to indicate a toxic *Amanita*, the mushroom is good.

Best time: July through October.

Status: Common and plentiful.

Tools needed: Basket, cloth bag.

Storage: Fresh mushrooms keep well in refrigerator when covered. Freezes well. Would also lend itself to home-canning method of preservation.

The Species

Ranked "choice" by most mushroom fans, gem-studded puffballs have a milder, sweeter flavor than their larger cousins, the giant puffballs. While it doesn't hurt to remove the somewhat tough outer coating on older specimens, it isn't really necessary because when cut in half and fried, the outer coating is not noticeable.

For many, including the author, this is the first mushroom of the year. Beginning any time after the Fourth of July, mushroom hunters keep their eyes open for gem-studded puffballs. While these delicious mushrooms grow in a variety of habitats, one often overlooked place is the land around old or disused gravel pits. Here, the puffballs grow out in the open, both in direct sun and in shade and partial shade.

While it is possible to locate a fairly large commune, or group of gem-studded puffballs, they more often appear here and there. This means that most times, the forager gets enough for one or two good meals and that is it. The author, despite being familiar with gem-studded puffballs for many years, rarely needs to worry about cooking and freezing gem-studded puffballs because most of what he collects gets eaten quickly, leaving few, if any, to put in storage.

So given their excellent flavor and widespread distribution, gem-studded puffballs are a very desirable mushroom. But in addition to their culinary value, gem-studded puffballs perform another valuable function, that is, the spores act as a styptic, a substance used to stanch bleeding.

RECIPE

Tom's Fried and Floured Gem-Studded Puffballs

After spreading gem-studded puffballs out on a table for inspection, make sure to remove, with a sharp knife or shears, the somewhat pointed holdfast at the bottom of the mushroom. Then cut enough mushrooms in half for one meal. Place a handful of white flour in a paper bag and then drop the mushrooms in. Hold the top of the bag to your mouth and gently blow, as if blowing up a balloon. Twist the bag top and shake the bag until the mushrooms are completely covered with a fine layer of flour.

Next, warm butter or margarine in a frying pan and add the mushrooms. Don't add too many at one time, though, because that makes it difficult to turn them. With heat on medium, keep turning the mushrooms until the cut half becomes golden brown. Serve immediately while piping hot.

Gem-studded puffballs

The author learned of this from an old dairy farmer who, after explaining how gem-studded puffballs were used to stop bleeding on livestock wounds, reached up over a rafter in his barn and pulled out a dried, gem-studded puffball. The farmer explained that in the past, farmers saved every dried puffball they could find and stored them at easily accessible locations in their barns.

RECIPE

Mushroom-Stuffed Tomatoes

Wash tomatoes, remove core and seeds from stem end. Cut or chop mushrooms up fine and stuff them into tomatoes. Sprinkle a bit of salt and pepper on top of mushrooms. In a bowl, put a handful of bread crumbs and pour on them one tablespoon of melted butter or margarine. Heap the bread crumbs over the tomatoes. Place stuffed tomatoes in a greased baking dish, add the balance of the bread crumbs by scattering between the tomatoes and heat in a moderate oven for 1 hour, checking after a half hour has passed. Make sure not to let the topping scorch.

Humans, too, can use gem-studded puffballs for a similar purpose. The author keeps one or two dried gem-studded puffballs in his medicine cabinet to stop razor cuts from bleeding. The way to use the mushrooms is to hold between fingers, pointing the top opening toward and holding it close to the cut, and squeezing quickly. When done properly, a puff of dark "smoke" shoots out and lands on the cut, halting bleeding. The spores are sterile, which is why these mushrooms are so handy for use as a styptic agent.

GIANT PUFFBALL
Calvatia gigantea

Synonym: Pasture puffball.

Identification: Large, round or slightly out-of-round, white. Clear-white inside and when sliced longitudinally has texture resembling cheese. A young *Amanita* sliced in this manner would show a developing cap and stem. But if the mushroom inside is plain white, then it is an edible puffball. The surface is smooth when young, but becomes cracked with age. Giant puffballs are among the most easily identified mushrooms.

Habitat: Appears, sometimes overnight, on lawns, grassy areas, and sometimes in pastures.

Use: Cooked.

Range: Throughout Maine anywhere preferred habitat exists.

Similarity to toxic species: A very small giant puffball may, when very young, resemble a developing toxic *Amanita* mushroom. The only way to tell the difference is to slice longitudinally, and if the flesh appears solid white, like cheese, the mushroom is a puffball.

Best time: August through October.

Status: Common.

Tools needed: None needed for picking, but a large potato or onion sack helps hold mushrooms if more than one are found.

Storage: When peeled and sliced, will remain for several days in the refrigerator if covered. Best used fresh, since giant puffballs become strongly flavored when frozen.

The Species

Giant puffballs appear suddenly, sometimes overnight. Although it is tempting to wait for the mushroom to reach its full potential in size, smaller or medium-sized, as in the size of a softball, are better eating. At maximum size, these become larger than a person's head, and sometimes as large as a soccer ball. And they have a stronger flavor than smaller specimens.

Not every lawn or pasture has these giant mushrooms, and the author considers himself fortunate that so many friends and neighbors are willing to share the giant puffballs that appear on their lawns every year in late summer. The author's lawn does not have any giant puffballs, and in an effort to get them established, he has distributed spores all over his lawn. Despite years of this treatment, no giant puffballs have yet appeared.

RECIPE

Because giant puffballs are so large and can be used in so many ways, here are three of the author's favorite recipes, plus one the author just discovered, puffball pizza.

Tom's Fried Puffball Bits

Here's a recipe that results in a product that can be used alone as a side dish or sprinkled on other foods such as steak or chicken.

As with many large puffballs, the outside skin must be peeled before use. We might liken this to peeling a giant boiled egg. With thumb and forefinger, try pinching a large section of mushroom. This cracks the skin and from there it is easy to pry off smaller pieces. When the mushroom is entirely peeled, then slice it into rounds and then chop the rounds into small bits using a chopping knife or even a kraut cutter.

Now put a heaping tablespoon of margarine in a small pan and fry to a golden brown, stirring frequently. Place on paper towel to dry and cool. The author often prepares these as nibbles, or snacks. Be careful when trying this, because it's hard to eat just one.

Giant puffball sliced and ready to cook

Grilled, Marinated Puffballs

Giant puffballs are like sponges in that they can soak up a huge volume of liquid. Taking advantage of that attribute, we can marinate giant puffball slices the same as we would any other food. Choice of marinade is a personal matter, although the author enjoys any salad dressing made with balsamic vinegar.

In a large bowl, pour in enough marinade to cover the bottom, and then lay the mushroom rounds down on top of it. From then on, depending upon how many rounds are to be cooked, pour more marinade on top of the mushrooms already in the bowl and place another slice (or slices) on top, alternating with layers of mushroom and marinade.

Allow the mushroom to marinate for at least 3 hours, and then cook on an outdoor grill at low heat. When almost done, so that a fork pierces it easily, turn the heat up to medium-high in order to slightly brown the outside. Serve immediately.

Tom and giant puffballs

A friend of the author's, though, has also spread spores on his lawn, with positive results. This begs the question, is the introduction of spores responsible, or would giant puffballs have appeared there anyway?

One aspect regarding foraging for giant puffballs is that the mushrooms can be seen from far away—the softball-sized, white mushroom standing out in sharp contrast to the green of a pasture or lawn.

Giant puffballs, besides being easily recognized, are quite dependable and usually appear in the same location every year. One of the author's best spots, a semishady area on the edge of a friend's lawn, often yields three or four huge mushrooms every year. Given the great size of giant puffballs, and given that they become strong when fried, cooled, and stored in the freezer, it is plain that more than one giant puffball at a time is more than enough for one person to deal with. So if finding a good supply of giant puffballs, consider this before harvesting them. A mushroom forager with a number of mushroom-loving friends can probably handle any number of giant puffballs. A lone individual might want to take just one or perhaps several smaller mushrooms.

PEAR-SHAPED PUFFBALL
Lycoperdon pyriforme

Identification: This is another puffball that is easily identified. First, its shape is significant. It is, as the common name denotes, pear-shaped. Or, we could also liken the shape to a hot-air balloon. Viewing a large number of these mushrooms on a decaying stump, we are reminded of a large group of balloons, all ready to take off. And like the gem-studded puffball, it has warts, but on this mushroom they are very small. The mushroom is off-white, tending toward brown. The mushrooms have small, thin rhizomorphs, or holdfasts, that look like tiny, white roots.

Habitat also helps in identifying pear-shaped puffballs. They are mostly found in shaded woodlands growing on stumps, rotting logs, and other types of decaying wood.

Habitat: Decaying wood.

Use: Cooked.

Range: Throughout Maine.

Similarity to toxic species: None.

Best time: August through October.

Status: Common and widespread.

Tools needed: Collecting basket, canvas bag.

Storage: Lasts several days in refrigerator. Keep covered.

The Species

While out in the field (or in this case, the forest) looking for mushrooms to photograph for this book, things were not going well for the author. The only mushrooms in evidence were either toxic or inedible. It looked like a lost day. But then a group of what looked like some kind of puffballs on an old, decaying

Pear-shaped mushrooms cooked in butter

RECIPE

Tom's Floured Puffballs

The same recipes that work for gem-studded puffballs work as well with this skull-shaped variety. That said, the author's favorite way of having pear-shaped puffballs is to cut each mushroom in half, roll it in flour, and fry in butter or margarine. You may also use the method described for gem-studded puffballs: Place a handful of white flour in a paper bag and drop the mushrooms in. Gather the top of the bag and gently blow into it, as if blowing up a balloon. Twist the bag top and shake the bag until the mushrooms are completely covered with a fine layer of flour. Fry as desired.

stump popped into view. Upon close inspection, the mushrooms proved to be pear-shaped puffballs.

After photographing the mushrooms, the problem of what to do with them presented itself. This was a photo-taking adventure, not a foraging trip. But where there is a will, there is a way, and these choice mushrooms went into jacket pockets. It was tough to get them all in, but in the end, tenacity won over.

This was a case of the author not following his own advice, which is "always carry something to collect mushrooms in, since there's no telling when or where you'll find them."

So to readers, it doesn't take much effort to carry a canvas bag around. They fold up nicely and don't take up much space. It would be a pity to let a number of meals' worth of delicious, choice mushrooms go to waste. You can bet that the author won't go on any more photography trips without bringing some sort of vessel to put good mushrooms in.

2 Gilled Mushrooms

FAIRY RING MUSHROOM
Marasmius oreades

Identification: This mushroom typically grows in a ring, or "fairy ring." Fairy ring mushrooms live out in the open on grassy surfaces. Look for them on lawns, golf courses, and meadows with short grass.

Identification, as with every other wild mushroom, is critical, since *M. oreades* could be confused with several toxic mushrooms. But fairy ring mushrooms have several distinguishing characteristics, one of them being quite unusual. That is, the gills, which are of an off-white color and wide set, are deep, ballooning out, giving the impression that they are under pressure and squatting out from the bottom of the cap.

Mature mushrooms, which some say smell like garlic or almonds, have a brownish cap, with a small bump in the center. Cap and stem are of a similar shade. The cap leaves a white, tending to buff, spore print. The stem is very tough and durable.

Also note that older, somewhat dried fairy ring mushrooms become rehydrated after a summer rain.

Habitat: Lawns, golf courses, open meadows, parks.
Use: Cooked, dried.
Range: Throughout Maine anywhere suitable habitat exists.
Similarity to toxic species: *Clitocybe dealbata*, another fungus that grows on lawns, often near fairy ring mushrooms. But on *C. sudorifica*, the gills grow partway down the stem.
Best time: June through September.
Status: Common and widespread.
Tools needed: Collecting basket.

Fairy ring mushrooms

Fairy ring mushrooms cap and gills

Storage: Will last several days in refrigerator if kept covered and stored loosely. If drying for storage, note that fairy rings dry easily, since they do not contain as much water as other mushrooms. Also, they keep longer when dried.

The Species

Where is the person who has not seen these mushrooms growing in their fairy rings on lawns and other grassy areas? This distinctive growth habit makes these among the most familiar mushrooms. After making a proper identification, fairy ring mushrooms are easily spotted. However, any mushroom or edible plant growing on lawns is susceptible to becoming tainted by pet urine or toxic lawn chemicals. People who find fairy ring mushrooms growing on their lawn would do well to take pains that their cat or dog stays away from the mushrooms.

MEADOW MUSHROOM
Agaricus campestris

Synonym: Pink bottom.

Identification: This mushroom perfectly illustrates the need to pick the entire mushroom, including every bit of stalk, for a valid identification. In order to differentiate *A. campestris* from the deadly toxic *Amanita virosa*, we need to inspect the bottom of the stalk. If it has a bulbous appearance, discard it immediately. Also, *A. virosa* has white gills at maturity.

The gills of *A. campestris* are somewhat white when very young, going to a pinkish hue (thus the other common name) and, finally, black at maturity.

Also, *A. campestris* has free, closely set gills. The cap is 2 or 3 inches in diameter and is usually white but may tend toward brown in some specimens. The cap is also dry to the touch and may exhibit a scaly nature.

Immature specimens of *A. campestris* go through the "button" stage. As the mushroom develops and the cap widens, a thin, whitish tissue connecting the cap to the stalk breaks, leaving a fragile ring on the stalk and a fringed appearance to the edge of the cap.

Meadow mushroom leaves a dark brown spore print.

Meadow mushroom cap, right, spore print, left

Habitat: Soaking rains help to bring out meadow mushrooms on open, grassy areas. Lawns are good places to look, as are cut-over meadows. This habit of growing out in the open helps to distinguish meadow mushrooms from deadly *A. virosa*, which don't usually grow in open areas but rather in mixed-growth forests and monoculture hardwood stands. Meadow mushrooms are usually available throughout the summer in Maine.

Range: Throughout Maine wherever lawns, pastures, and meadows are found.

Meadow mushrooms

Meadow mushrooms ready for cooking

Similarity to toxic species: A careless collector, failing to harvest the entire mushroom, including the beneath-the-ground part of the stalk, could confuse meadow mushroom with deadly toxic *A. virosa*.

Best time: From late May through August.

Status: Common.

Tools needed: A hand trowel may come in handy for digging up the stem. A basket serves as the best possible method for carrying and a canvas bag rates as a good second choice.

Storage: Meadow mushroom is closely related to *Agaricus bisporus*, the mushrooms we buy in the stores. Consequently, meadow mushroom has a similar shelf life when refrigerated. These can easily stay in the refrigerator for two or three days without losing much in the way of quality.

The Species

Meadow mushrooms are another of those kinds that accomplished mushroom hunters can spot while driving along the road in a motor vehicle. That's not to say that we shouldn't go through all the steps in the identification process. But knowing the general appearance of meadow mushrooms from a distance and

---

RECIPE

Steak and Meadow Mushrooms

Just as commercially grown mushrooms pair well with beefsteak, wild meadow mushrooms serve this purpose even better. And while meadow mushrooms do hold up to storage, they are never better than when fresh picked. Unfortunately for commercial mushrooms, that just can't happen, and goodness knows how many days might have elapsed since the commercial mushrooms were harvested, packaged, shipped, displayed on the store's shelf, and bought by the customer.

Being meaty and solid, meadow mushroom works best when cut into thin to medium slices. If the steak is to be grilled or broiled, cook the cut-up mushrooms in a separate pan at low to medium heat, reserving the cooking liquid. After the steak is done and has sat for a minute or so, pour the cooked mushrooms and liquid over it.

However, if cooking the steak in a pan (preferably a cast-iron frying pan), cook the mushrooms in the same pan. Put the mushrooms in the pan first and cook until about half-done, perhaps for several minutes. Then move mushrooms to one edge of the pan, turn up the heat and cook the steak.

Those who eschew meat can make a fine side dish of cut-up, fried meadow mushrooms.

---

being familiar with their favored habitat helps to locate these common mushrooms of summer in Maine.

The author has had meadow mushrooms appear only sparsely and at odd intervals on his own lawn, but the lawn of a public school 5 miles away has a much more dependable crop.

Many times it is possible to find meadow mushrooms at all different stages of development in the same location. This is a great help in identification.

Even if only two or three meadow mushrooms are available from your favorite mushroom lawn or meadow, pick them and take them home, since two or three of the larger meadow mushrooms are enough for an ample side dish for one person.

MICA CAP
Coprinus micaceus

Synonym: Glistening coprinus.

Identification: The small, brown-buff cap has several distinguishing features. First, young specimens are covered with small, fine particles, and these particles are reflective, much as are small mica particles (thus the common name). Also, the cap has striations, or furrows. In mature specimens, the cap appears to hang, loosely, in the manner of a kilt or skirt. The gills are white when young, later changing to dark gray-brown, close-set and attached. The fragile, hollow stem is whitish and runs from 2 to 3 inches long.

Habitat: Grows in clumps around trees, tree roots, and even fenceposts and also from decaying, buried wood.

Use: Cooked.

Range: Throughout Maine.

Similarity to toxic species: Resembles the inky cap mushroom, *Coprinus atramentarius*. The inky cap when mature may have a covering of silky fibers, or scales. Inky caps are considered edible with caution; it is advised not to consume alcohol for one or two days before or after ingesting *C. atramentarius* in order to circumvent an unpleasant but nonfatal reaction. Since there are several small, brown Coprinus, look carefully for small, brown reflective particles on the cap.

Best time: Spring and again in fall.

Mica caps

Status: Common and widespread.

Tools needed: Basket.

Storage: This is one mushroom where storage is not a consideration because if stored in the refrigerator, the mushroom turns into a black, sticky ooze overnight. So make sure to cook mica caps soon after picking.

The Species

The author's first encounter with mica cap mushrooms was over 20 years ago. A number of these mushrooms had popped up on the soft shoulder along the

---

RECIPE

Mica Caps on Toast

Sure, mica caps can stand on their own when fried in butter, oil, or margarine and served as a side dish. But since the mushrooms generate quite a bit of liquid on their own, they can stand as a main dish when served on toast and accompanied by spring-time (or fall) side dishes such as asparagus or spinach.

driveway. Some had already decomposed as evidenced by little black piles of sticky, viscous matter. But there were enough mushrooms in their prime left for one good meal.

These, when sautéed in a little butter, were very tasty. It was hard to reconcile the delicious mushrooms in the frying pan with those piles of black ooze outside. But everything organic eventually decays, and these mushrooms simply decay faster than most anything else.

Mica caps are said to return to the same spot every year for a number of years. Oddly, the mushroom stand along the author's driveway was a one-time proposition. Perhaps that had something to do with the gravel driveway being new. It had only been built the year before.

Anyway, after 20-some years of checking, the mica caps have never returned. But that doesn't pose a big problem because these mushrooms are wide-scattered and very cosmopolitan. Anyone with an eye for mushrooms should be able to spot mica caps growing while walking, hiking, or even driving down the road in a motor vehicle.

Because of their ephemeral nature, mica caps should be considered a special treat, something to be enjoyed in season, when and wherever they are found.

OYSTER MUSHROOM
Pleurotus ostreatus

JIM MEUNINCK

Identification: Oyster mushrooms are so-called because of the shape of their cap, which some say resembles an oyster shell. Gills vary from close-set to wide. Gills, like the cap, are white (although some are on the grayish side). The gills run down the stalk.

The stalk, what there is of it, is very short and serves mostly as a holdfast, securing the mushroom to the host tree and acting as a vehicle for nutrients.

Oyster mushroom caps are usually about 2 inches in diameter, although some can grow to 12 inches across. The author has never seen caps of that size, and readers should not expect to either.

Foragers may confuse oyster mushrooms with angel's wings, *Pleurocybella porrigens*. However, angel's wings mostly grow on decomposing hemlock trees or stumps. Also, angel's wings lack a stalk. Even if these two mushrooms were collected at the same time, it would be okay since angel's wings are edible. Oyster mushroom makes a pale lilac spore print. Note that some years ago, a group of people in Japan were poisoned on angel wing mushrooms. However, other facts were possibly involved. Angel wings are still noted as edible in field guides. Oyster mushrooms may also be confused with *Crepidatus applanatus*, but the latter are small and leave a brown spore print.

Habitat: Found mostly on hardwood trees, most commonly sugar maples with the bark still attached. Both live and dead/decomposing trees can be hosts.

Use: Cooked, dried.

Range: Throughout Maine.

Similarity to toxic species: None.

Best time: While oyster mushrooms can grow year-round under favorable conditions, August through November is the best time for Maine foragers.

Status: Common, but requires considerable searching. When located, a good spot can give up several pounds of mushrooms.

Tools needed: Pick mushrooms from host tree by hand and place loosely in a collecting basket.

Storage: Will keep for several days in refrigerator. Freezes well and can be dried.

The Species

While taste is subjective, most mushroom fans rate oyster mushrooms as choice. Oysters are among the author's favorite wild mushrooms. Many years ago a colony of oysters appeared near a small stream on the author's woodlot. These were dependable mushrooms, giving several good meals' worth each year.

Oyster mushroom   JIM MEUNINCK

Oyster mushroom JIM MEUNINCK

RECIPE

Oyster Mushrooms on Grouse Breast

Oyster mushrooms are often at their best in October and early November. This coincides with the hunting season for ruffed grouse. The author's dream meal consists of sautéed grouse breasts covered with oyster mushrooms.

When the breasts (chicken breast can be substituted) are cooked about halfway through, start the mushrooms in a separate pan. Use either a nonscorching margarine or an unflavored cooking oil such as canola oil. Get the oil hot and drop in the mushrooms. Larger mushrooms might need to be cut in half or even quartered, and small ones can go in whole. Stir while cooking and when both grouse breasts and mushrooms are done, serve by spreading the cooked oyster mushrooms over the breasts.

Rice is optional, but if using rice, choose a white variety for color contrast. Add a side dish of foraged greens (dandelion greens become mild in fall after the first few frosts) and the meal is complete. Choice of wine is optional, but the author favors a good Merlot or Chianti. Others may opt for a white wine.

Oyster mushrooms

But the stump was not as reliable as the mushrooms that lived on and in it. It eventually decayed and returned to the ground, and the oyster mushrooms disappeared along with it.

Interestingly, oyster mushrooms are one kind that some foragers pick for the market. This presents an interesting situation for those who are unfamiliar with oyster mushrooms (or any other kind of wild mushroom). Here, with a nametag and price, are some excellent wild mushrooms. As an exercise in mushroom identification, then, first ascertain from the store that these are, in fact, oyster mushrooms. Then buy a small amount, take them home and pretend that they are a new, unfamiliar mushroom. Check them against photos and descriptions in a mushroom field guide. Go through the entire process, including making a spore print. Intense scrutiny will reveal that yes, these are oyster mushrooms. It also means that from that time on, identifying oyster mushrooms will be considerably easier.

This tactic presents itself as a safe way to get hands-on experience identifying wild mushrooms. Fortunately, oyster mushrooms are a favorite of buyers, and many supermarkets and health food stores carry them.

Like any other gilled mushroom, oyster mushrooms collect debris in their gills. So here again, it pays to use a scrupulously clean collecting basket. If using a canvas bag, make sure it is freshly washed.

SHAGGY MANE
Coprinus comatus

Synonym: Lawyer's wig, barrister's wig.

Identification: Shaggy mane caps resemble elongated eggs, with a shaggy or scaly exterior. White overall, the cap and stem combination looks like a giant cotton swab, one end stuck in the ground. The cap never becomes flattened or widely spread as with other cap-type mushrooms. In order to view the gills, the cap must be lifted, something like a skirt. The gills are closely set and white when young, turning pinkish as the mushroom ages. When the mushroom is entirely spent, the gills turn into a black, gooey mass. The stalk may be as long as 8 inches, although it's usually somewhat less than half that. The stalk is hollow and has a delicate ring near its base.

Habitat: Lawns; open, grassy areas; gravelly areas; and hard-packed dirt.

Use: Cooked.

Range: Throughout Maine.

Similarity to toxic species: None.

Best time: September and October, may persist into November.

Status: Common.

Tools needed: Basket, cloth bag, small cardboard box.

Storage: Best if eaten shortly after picking, but will keep 24 hours in a refrigerator if placed in waxed paper, a waxed bag, or a brown bag. However, some quality will be lost.

The Species

Shaggy mane has a special place in the author's heart, since it was the very first wild mushroom he located and identified on his own. This was in September on a grassy area on the edge of Penobscot Bay in Rockland.

Upon seeing these mushrooms, there was little doubt as to what species they were, since nothing else looks exactly like them. The common names of lawyer's wig and barrister's wig immediately came to mind. All the same, the mushrooms were carefully picked, taken home, and compared to photos in several mushroom guides.

After that initial experience, shaggy manes began showing up in various places, some quite unexpected. For instance, the causeway bridging the Searsport mainland and Sears Island has gravel shoulders. And one year, shaggy mane mushrooms grew on these hard-packed, gravelly spots. The problem, though, when foraging on public land such as this, is that people come here specifically

Shaggy mane mushrooms

RECIPE

Tom's Shaggy Manes over Rice

Some mushrooms lend themselves to drying, but shaggy manes are not among them. The way to cook shaggy manes is to slowly simmer them in a frying pan. The author prefers a cast-iron pan for all mushroom cooking.

After removing by hand any grass, sticks, or other debris that might cling to the mushrooms, warm a small quantity of cooking oil in the pan. Then, before adding the shaggy manes, gently crush each mushroom by hand so that it flattens out. This helps it cook through better. Simmer the mushrooms for 2 or 3 minutes and wait for them to produce a black liquid. This broth captures the essence of the mushroom and should be served with it.

Any table grade red wine, while not necessary, will add to the overall taste of shaggy manes. Use only a little, perhaps half a shot glass.

When the mushrooms are cooked through, serve mushrooms and broth over basmati or jasmine white rice. Some fresh garden vegetables and a salad complement this meal of shaggy mane mushrooms.

to walk their dogs, and the prospect of eating any mushroom soiled by someone's dog is disconcerting, to say the least.

Shaggy manes usually grow in groups, which can include large numbers of individual mushrooms.

While September is usually the best time in Midcoast Maine, shaggy manes may show up in late August in northern Maine and not until late September and early October in southern Maine.

Here's another tip that is specific to shaggy mane mushrooms. If you find a quantity of shaggy manes nearby, don't pick them until it's almost time to cook them. That way they will remain fresh and at their peak. The reason for this is that shaggy mane mushrooms, if kept in storage for more than one day, will darken and dissolve. Of all foods that really should be eaten fresh, shaggy mane mushrooms top the list.

YELLOW WAXY CAP
Hygrocybe flavescens

Synonym: Golden waxy cap.

Identification: A small, up to 3-inch-tall orange mushroom with edge of cap tending toward yellowish. Cap is 1 to 2¾ inches wide. Cap generally flat but can have either a sunken center or a slight bulge. Center of cap darker orange than the rest. Young specimens sticky, becoming dry as mushroom ages. Also orange at first, yellowing with age. Attached gills also thick, often seen hanging down below cap in a manner similar to fairy ring, *Marasmius oreades*. Stalk is yellow, the same as the cap, but has a white base. Makes a white spore print. **Note that even with the stated description, waxy cap is a difficult mushroom to identify. Some authorities dislike the taste and others note that eating this mushroom makes them ill. Be very careful when dealing with this beautiful mushroom.** However, even if you don't eat it, it is nice to be able to identify this brightly colored mushroom.

Habitat: Woodland floor, on leaf litter and mossy areas. Common in mixed-growth woodlands.

Use: Cooked.

Range: Throughout Maine.

Similarity to toxic species: None, except some other *Hygrocybes* can be quite bitter.

Best time: One of this small mushroom's biggest selling points is that it becomes available in June and can last into November.

Status: Common.

Tools needed: Collecting basket or cloth bag.

Storage: Best fresh, but will keep in refrigerator for several days.

The Species

Many foragers consider yellow waxy cap mushrooms too small to be of much consequence. But since they often appear in great numbers, the sheer volume compensates for the mushroom's small size.

Yellow waxy caps and other members of the *Hygrocybe* family are easy to locate because of their bright color. Also, yellow waxy caps are fairly common. They often appear in early summer, making them one of the few early edible mushrooms.

The author first became aware of yellow waxy caps while walking through a seldom-visited part of his woodlot. There were only a few mushrooms, but that was enough to elicit interest. Yellow waxy caps touch upon another important aspect of mushroom harvesting, that being the most valuable mushrooms are

Yellow waxy cap group

Scrambled Yellow Waxy Caps with Bacon Bits

On the lowest possible heat setting, slowly cook three or four strips of bacon, turning as needed. The bacon should be uniformly brown and crisp. Remove bacon from pan and replace it with bits of broken or chopped yellow waxy caps. Raise heat to medium-low and stir frequently until mushrooms are thoroughly cooked. Mix cooked mushroom with bacon bits and serve as a side to any breakfast dish. Can also serve as a side dish to any meal.

those that we can find near home. Mushrooms found on the forager's own property or on land where permission to harvest is given can become a regular part of the forager's year.

It seems fair to say that dependable, easily located edible mushrooms, no matter the species, are valuable assets to any forager. Yellow waxy caps surely fit into this category.

3 Polyporales

ARTIST'S CONK
Ganoderma applanatum

JIM MEUNINCK

Synonym: None known.

Identification: Brown top, kidney or semicircle shape, hard like wood. Stem short and stout where it attaches to dead hardwood trees. Cap can measure up to 24 inches at widest point. Brown on top with bumps and concentric rings, or zones. White on bottom, or pore side.

Habitat: Found on living and dead hardwood trees. The mushroom attaches directly to the trees, as it lacks a stem.

Use: Dried pore side is quite smooth and, when fresh picked, can be carved or engraved. When fully dried, pore side serves as an artist's palette. Gift shops throughout Maine sell artist's conks with paintings on their pore side. Artist's conk also has reputed antibacterial qualities and some people grind the mushroom up for use as a tea. Do not use internally without first discussing with a doctor, since components in the mushroom may interact with prescription medications.

Range: Throughout Maine in woodlands.

Similarity to toxic species: None.

Best time: Available year-round, but best in late summer and early fall when brown spores collect on top of cap.

Status: Common.

Tools needed: Can often be broken from tree simply by holding firm and wiggling one way then the other. Some may require a hatchet to separate from host tree.
Storage: Store in a dry setting.

The Species

Artist conks are a standard fixture on tables and shelves in Maine's woodland and lakeshore cabins and cottages. Being hard and very dense, these shelf-type mushrooms last for many years. Some people apply a coat of varnish to the top as a further preservation measure.

If harvesting artist's conk for carving or etching, take great care not to touch the white bottom, since even slight pressure will discolor it. If harvesting to paint, touching the bottom is not a problem.

Another, similar polypore, red-belted polypore, *Fomitopsis pinicola*, has a deep red band near the cap edge, or margin. It, too, can be used the same as artist's conk. Red-belted polypores grow to a large size, just like artist's conks.

Artist's conk, pore side JIM MEUNINCK

CHAGA
Inonotus obliquus

Synonym: King of medicinal mushrooms, mushroom of immortality, clinker polypore, birch canker polypore.

Identification: Chaga looks much like burnt residue on the side of a tree. And since it takes many forms, it has no definite structure. However, chaga looks much like a cinder, and for those old enough to remember the age of steam, chaga looks very much like "clinkers," the residue of coal burning left alongside railroad tracks. Chaga is black on the outside and dirty-yellow inside.

Habitat: Chaga grows on white (paper) and yellow birch, sometimes singly and sometimes in multiples.

Use: Chaga is ground quite fine and made into a medicinal tea. Also made into alcohol-based tinctures.

Range: Throughout Maine.

Similarity to toxic species: None. However, some have mistakenly collected black knot, *Apiosponna morbosum*, from cherry trees and were sickened. Stick to collecting from birch trees.

Tools needed: Hammer, chisel, basket or canvas collecting bag.

Storage: Chaga can be stored in container in a dry closet. The author stores his chaga in a zip-style freezer bag in the freezer, believing that freezing helps to preserve the mushroom's potency.

The Species

The author, like so many others, only recently discovered chaga. For some years, participants on the author's wild plant field trips asked about chaga, and when a fellow outdoor writer began espousing chaga's health benefits, it seemed that the time had come to sit down and learn just what this near-mythical mushroom looked like and where to find it.

Claims regarding chaga's health-boosting properties were legion, but still it seemed doubtful that all these were true. No one has yet found the universal panacea for every ill, but the vast number of claims made on behalf of chaga make it seem as if this quirky-looking mushroom has more going for it than meets the eye.

And even if only a small percentage of the claims regarding chaga are true, it would represent a great source of natural medicine. But in order to ingest chaga a person must first find chaga. So finding that chaga grows on both white (paper)

Chaga on birch tree

and yellow birch, and having a woodlot full of both species, it was time to go on a chaga hunt.

It didn't take long to spot a rectangle-shaped, black, burnt-looking mass only several feet off the ground on a white birch. With snow on the ground the white-on-black contrast was greatly reinforced.

The chaga felt hard and woody to the touch, and in fact, chaga is very dense and heavy for its size. A solid tap with a hammer dislodged the chaga from its host tree. Little fine bits of chaga fell to the ground, giving the snow a look of being sprinkled with ground, black pepper. Note that when harvesting chaga, any remaining parts can regenerate and can be harvested again in from three to 10 years.

Since chaga is reportedly at its most potent after a month of 30-degree Fahrenheit temperatures, it is probably best harvested in late fall or early winter. But here again, it's hard to pinpoint the source of this knowledge. It seems likely that any time you find chaga, it will contain beneficial properties.

Chaga has a long history in eastern countries and in much of Europe. Russia, in particular, has a long-established affinity for chaga, and reports of super-athletes who attribute their incredible physical abilities to chaga use are common.

To learn more about chaga's health-lifting properties, just do an Internet search. The list of chaga health benefits is long, and the list of its components is even longer. As a result, numbers of companies, mostly the same companies that sell medicinal herbs, have come up with a list of health-giving properties as long as a person's arm.

But at the same time, many of these companies extol other natural herbs and products, and while many of the claims are probably correct, it seems unlikely that they all are. This brings up the question of healthy skepticism. If planning to harvest and use chaga, ask your medical doctor before beginning. With any product that has so many varied components, a possibility exists that one of more of these components may adversely react with prescription medicines or existing medical conditions. Do not use chaga without consulting a medical doctor.

But if the doctor provides an approval, it's time to start using this special, un-mushroom-like mushroom. Here is the author's method of preparing and using chaga.

RECIPE

Chaga Medicinal Tea

Because chaga comes from the tree in a state that cannot be used as is, it must be broken down in some way. The author likes to break off small pieces with a tack hammer and then make them into a coarse powder or grainy substance with the use of a kitchen grater. Some people put broken-up bits of chaga in their blender to make a finer product.

After this, a teaspoon of ground chaga added to a cup of boiling water makes the finished product. The longer the chaga steeps, the stronger, and, presumably the more beneficial, the tea.

Some people put their ground chaga in a tea ball or some other type of strainer. It is also possible to simply pour boiling water on the ground chaga and then wait for suspended particles to sink to the bottom.

Chaga tea is said to have a vanilla-like flavor, but the author instead notes a pronounced maple flavor. As just a tea taken for the soothing pleasure of a hot, flavorful drink, chaga excels. And given its various, purported beneficial properties, a chaga habit may be one that people wish to develop.

Chaga is also made into an extract, but the process is somewhat complicated and too long to outline here. But as its use in a tea is the most common way to take chaga, suffice it to say that drinking a cup of chaga tea daily is a perfectly fine way to use this mushroom.

CHICKEN OF THE WOODS
Laetiporus sulphureus

Synonym: Sulphur shelf, chicken mushroom.

Identification: A shelf-type mushroom that grows on hardwood trees, particularly oak, ash, and cherry. Rarely grows on softwood. Chicken mushrooms grow one upon the other, like overlapping brackets. There is no stalk, but the part where a stalk would be attaches directly to the substrate, or host tree.

The top of the cap is orange, except the cap edge is yellow. The top of the cap, especially on young, tender specimens, sometimes has a waxy feel. The underside of the cap is also yellow (thus the allusion to sulphur), but may rarely be white. The underside of the cap has pores rather than gills. A young stand may consist of only a few mushrooms, but a more advanced colony may extend for many feet up the tree. Note that older specimens can cause illness. Look for young, pliable specimens.

Habitat: Living, dying, or compromised hardwood trees. Also on stumps and, rarely, even on roots.

Use: Cooked.

Range: Throughout Maine.

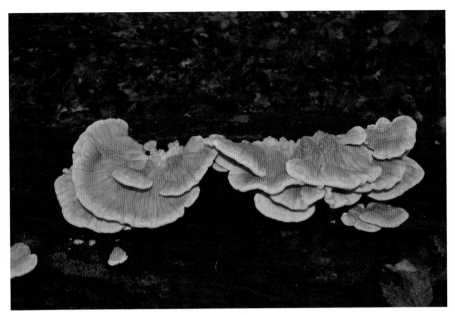

Chicken of the woods mushroom JIM MEUNINCK

Similarity to toxic species: A different species, *L. Huronesis*, may cause severe gastrointestinal distress. It is found on softwood trees and, except for identifying the host, is difficult to distinguish from *Sulphureus*.

Best time: September and October.

Status: Common and widespread.

Tools needed: Basket or cloth bag. In the instance of locating a large group of chicken mushrooms, two baskets or bags may be needed. When picking, just break off the mushrooms by hand. Any mushroom part remaining on the tree will be too tough to eat.

Storage: Keeps well in refrigerator and remains good for four or five days. Freezes well.

The Species

Chicken of the woods is one of the most easily identified mushrooms. The long, orange swath of color offered by a group of these mushrooms running up a tree can be spied even while driving down the highway at highway speed. Foragers walking in the woods specifically looking for chicken mushrooms usually spot them from a great distance away.

The author has had times when he had so many chicken mushrooms that it was difficult to find enough people to give them to. Some years, though, these mushrooms are scarce and any amount at all is carefully hoarded.

It is important to note that chicken mushrooms change appearance as they age. Young mushrooms are fan-shaped, with a rounded, smooth outside edge.

Chicken of the woods mushroom JIM MEUNINCK

RECIPE

Pan-Fried Chicken Mushrooms

The basic recipe calls for cutting tender parts of chicken mushroom caps into small bits and frying them in oil until just crisp. These can serve as a side dish to any meal or can be sprinkled on salads. In texture, fried chicken mushroom bits somewhat resemble bacon bits. The taste, though, does not remind one of chicken but rather of lobster.

A more elaborate recipe allows chicken mushrooms to shine. Gather:

1–2 tablespoon canola oil or mild olive oil
½ cup chopped chicken of the woods mushroom
½ cup sliced scallions
½ medium onion, minced
5 eggs, beaten
¼ cup Swiss cheese, shredded
Salt and pepper to taste

Heat the oil and add mushrooms, scallions, and onions. Cook at medium-high heat until mushrooms release their liquid. Reduce heat to medium and slowly add eggs, stirring constantly until eggs are almost set. Add cheese. Continue to stir and cook for 1 minute more. Add salt, pepper, or favorite seasoning (the author enjoys Slap Ya Mama Cajun seasoning) and serve immediately.

On older specimens the edge becomes wavy, even spiky, making the mushroom look very different from younger ones. Also, older mushrooms are mostly hard and tough except for the edges. In some cases, the forager is compelled to leave most of the cap on the tree, taking only the flexible, tender outside edges.

So it pays to harvest young mushrooms when and if possible. Also, as the mushrooms age, various insects attack the underside, and certain insect larvae even drill their way into the fleshy part of the cap. Once, the author picked a copious amount of chicken mushrooms and decided to share his good fortune with friends. The friends called back the next day, saying that while it was a nice gesture to give them mushrooms, they were full of tiny worms. Unfortunately, the author had already eaten several meals without noticing the infestation. From that day on, though, part of the harvesting process includes a close scrutiny of the underside of the cap and even the inner parts of a randomly selected cap in order to check for insects and other pests.

Most books list *L. sulphureus* as a perfectly safe mushroom, ideally suited for beginning foragers. But some people develop stomach problems and other distasteful symptoms. Scientists speculate that these scattered reactions may be due to something in the tree rather than in the mushrooms themselves. Either way, it is important for first-timers to eat only a small amount of the cooked mushroom in order to see if any reaction will occur. If all seems good the next day, it should be okay to try larger amounts.

HEN OF THE WOODS
Grifola frondosa

Synonym: Hen.

Identification: The overlapping caps of this brown-above and white-below mushroom, when seen from afar, suggest a red hen with her feathers ruffled. The caps have a smooth, rubbery feel and when bent down and then released, quickly spring back in place. The multibranched stalk is white, quite thick and short and stubby. A large mushroom, sometimes weighing 4 or 5 pounds.

Habitat: On oak stumps, usually red oak but will grow on other oaks as well. Also grown in soil atop buried roots of oak trees.

Use: Cooked.

Range: Throughout Maine.

Similarity to toxic species: None. However, *G. frondosa* is quite similar to the edible polypore *G. umbellata*. The caps on *G. umbellata* are umbrella-shaped and are more open than on *G. frondosa*.

Best time: September into early October.

Status: Despite being listed as a common mushroom, *G. frondosa* is not overly abundant.

Tools needed: Large basket or large cloth bag.

Storage: Fresh mushroom keeps well in refrigerator. Freezes well and, because of its considerable mass, would probably be a good candidate for home canning.

The Species

Hen of the woods mushrooms are eagerly sought by collectors. These large mushrooms, particularly those growing on oak stumps, usually return year after year. However, nothing is ever guaranteed in the world of wild mushroom harvesting, and some years hens fail to appear. But given the right conditions, a good balance of wet and dry weather without any significant droughts or flooding, a no-show hen may return the following year.

The author once had a "hen of the woods circuit," which he would visit each year in mid-September. However, since these were along public roads, the inevitable happened to each site. In one instance, the town dug up a row of buried stumps and installed a sidewalk. But these stump remnants were home to *G. frondosa* spawn and when the stumps went, so went the mushrooms.

Another spot, this one a large, fairly high stump along an unpaved rural road, was a hindrance to the snowplow, since the plow blade sometimes struck it. This was by far the most reliable producer of the biggest hens around. But because of the problems with the plow, an excavator was hauled in to dig out the stump.

And for some unknown reason, an oak stump that produced a huge hen about 12 years ago has not produced a single mushroom since. This is how the

---

RECIPE

Garden Vegetable Soup with Hen of the Woods Mushroom

When making a garden vegetable soup, begin with one 14½-ounce can of beef stock in a large saucepan. Add cut-up vegetables such as carrots, celery, potato, summer squash, green bean, sweet corn, chopped parsley, and any other fresh garden vegetable. While this slowly simmers, add ½ cup (or more to taste) hen of the woods mushroom.

Cook on low heat for 45 minutes. The author allows such soups to simmer on a woodstove in his cast-iron Dutch oven. Keep the top on the Dutch oven and the soup will mix itself as it condenses, collects on the convex top, and drips back onto itself. Cooking time for this can be from 45 minutes to several hours. The Dutch oven keeps moisture in, so the soup cannot evaporate no matter how long the oven is kept on top of the stove.

Hen of the woods mushroom fills Tom's kitchen table.

world of hen of the woods harvesting works. It's a here-today and gone-tomorrow situation. But as favorite sites are either destroyed or stop producing, new sites must be located.

Individual foragers have something else working against them. In recent years, commercial foragers have largely taken over many fine hen of the woods areas. This coincides with the growing popularity of restaurants that feature locally harvested and locally grown foods. But commercial harvesters can't possibly find all the hens, and enough are spared that individual foragers can still have their hen of the woods each fall.

Like favorite fishing holes and prime fiddlehead (young fronds of edible ferns) spots, hen of the woods sites are to be treasured, kept secret from all but the most devoted friends or family members. A friend once told the author how a visitor from Italy described the *G. frondosa* situation in his native country. There, the man said, people were extremely possessive of their hen sites, and it was rumored, he said, that episodes of violence erupted in disputes over hen of the woods territories.

Here in Maine, while hens are eagerly sought, mushroom hunters are more civil. And despite the mushroom's popularity among knowledgeable foragers, most people cannot identify a hen of the woods. Thus, many fine mushrooms are left to decompose naturally.

In the "Tools needed" line above, I suggest that foragers carry a large basket or cloth bag. That's because hen of the woods mushrooms are so huge. And not only huge, they are heavy. The author once located one of the biggest hens he had ever seen. This was at the bottom of a steep hill. The first step was to break the mushroom from the stump. That was accomplished by steadily pulling and twisting. After that, it was necessary to climb the hill and retrieve two baskets from the car.

The mushroom was so large that even being broken into sections, another trip was necessary to get the entire mushroom. And that second time walking up the hill with a basket made heavy with mushroom pieces was hard work. But the reward was well worth the effort. In addition to eating fresh hen of the woods mushrooms over the course of several days, the author was able to freeze a large amount and to give close friends each a sizeable portion.

Hen of the woods mushrooms are considered choice.

TURKEY TAIL
Trametes versicolor

JIM MEUNINCK

Synonym: None given.

Identification: Caps partially cupped, growing in concentric circles and rosettes, multi-colored zones on cap, yellowish pores on bottom of cap, with alternating textures from smooth to velvety as the colors change. A polypore, turkey tail has pores on bottom of cap. Leaves a cream, yellowish, or gray spore print.

Habitat: Grows on dead wood, mostly hardwood but sometimes on conifers. Often found on stumps or on wood lying on the ground.

Use: Turkey tails have medicinal value.

Range: Throughout Maine.

Similarity to toxic species: None known.

Best time: From midspring until early winter.

Status: Common.

Tools needed: Collecting basket, jackknife for cutting away from host.

Storage: Dry and store in airtight container.

The Species

One of the most common and certainly one of the most beautiful mushrooms, turkey tail mushroom is ubiquitous on dead wood. The flesh is tough and

Turkey tail mushroom

inedible, but that's not what turkey tail mushroom is about. Like chaga mushroom, turkey tail has a long history of medicinal use in other parts of the world, especially Asia.

One of the more interesting and, if true, invaluable attributes of turkey tail mushrooms is that they are said to cure some cancers and are an established part of cancer treatment in Asian countries.

Turkey tail mushrooms are so attractive, they have been used as earrings and as foils in various artistic endeavors. Turkey tail mushrooms are a natural dye.

RECIPE

Turkey Tail Tea

Turkey tails must be dried prior to use. An easy way to do this is to line the bottom of a basket with turkey tails and hang the basket in an airy, out-of-the way place. When they are fully dried, run the mushrooms through a blender to make a coarse powder. For a cup of turkey tail tea, use 1 teaspoon dried mushroom powder to 1 cup of hot water. Allow to steep.

Some people take turkey tail mushroom tea regularly in order to boost their immune system and keep it strong. But as with any herbal remedy, don't use turkey tail mushroom without checking with your medical doctor first.

4   Chanterelles

BLACK TRUMPET
Craterellus fallax

Synonym: Horn of plenty, death trumpet, cornucopia.

Identification: One of the easier mushrooms to identify. Black trumpets and their twin species, horn of plenty, *Craterellus cornucopioides*, are pretty much interchangeable for the mushroom hunter. Both have a funnel-shaped body with rudimentary gills running down the outside. The stem and body are all one piece, not separated as with many other mushrooms.

The tissue or body of black trumpets and horn of plenty, the part that forms the "horn," is very thin and a bit brittle. These mushrooms grow in huge colonies, so even though an individual mushroom has but little mass, the mushrooms more than make up for it in numbers and taste.

Both cap horn and attached stem are of one color. This can range from black to gray and even a light brown. So just look for small (2 to 3 inches tall) mushrooms growing on the ground in large groups. If they are trumpet or horned shape and very thin, they are one or the other of the above-named species.

Black trumpet and chanterelle mushrooms

Many mushroom hunters report sensing a strong, fruity smell, so intense that they often recognize black trumpets by smell before actually finding the mushrooms. The author finds these mushrooms only lightly aromatic, and at that, the aroma is reminiscent of fresh forest loam.

Black trumpet produces slightly pink spore prints, and horn of plenty drops spores that, while lacking in pigment, have an overall whitish look.

These small mushrooms do look like tiny horns of plenty. And the reference to them looking like a trumpet is well-founded. So when hunting, look for groups of mushrooms growing on the ground, with each mushroom looking like a little horn.

Finally, don't search for black trumpets out in the open, because they need shade or semishade from trees to live.

Habitat: On the forest floor in either hardwood or softwood forests. Often grows thickly on paths or disused wood roads.

Use: Cooked.

Range: Throughout Maine.

Similarity to toxic species: None, but both black trumpets and horn of plenty are often confused with each other. Since both are edible, that poses no problem.

Best time: From August into September. These mushrooms are easily killed by frost.

Status: Common and abundant.

Tools needed: Collecting basket. Make sure to bring a large basket, since black trumpets grow in large colonies.

Storage: Stores in refrigerator for up to one week. Be sure to keep covered or the mushrooms will dry out. A plastic bag works fine, but don't close it up too tightly, since that may cause the mushrooms to sweat. Also, black trumpets and horn of plenty dry well. When dried, these mushrooms will keep their flavor for a long time, perhaps even for several years.

The Species

The author feels blessed in having a woodlot with one section rich in black trumpets. It's an annual ritual to go out back sometime in mid- to late-August and hunt for black trumpets. These grow on an old, disused wood road. And even when the ground is littered with mushrooms for many feet around, they are not always easy to spot. Their short stature and subdued colors allow the mushrooms to blend in with dead leaves and sticks littering the forest floor.

The author's grandmother did him a great disservice many years ago when she pointed out deadly toxic "death trumpets." The scare worked and it wasn't until later in life that the author realized that these diminutive, horn-shaped mushrooms are not deadly poison but rather safe and delightful.

To be fair to grandma, many people from a few generations ago had phobias about "toadstools," or poison mushrooms. From a purely scientific point of view, mushrooms and toadstools are one and the same, but some are safe and edible, while others are toxic to one degree or another.

RECIPE

Black Trumpets on Steak

Black trumpets and horn of plenty mushrooms contain a surprising amount of liquid. This liquid expresses itself upon being placed in a frying pan and slowly cooked. So just use enough butter, margarine, or oil to keep mushrooms from sticking. They will produce a good quantity of their own black liquor as they cook.

Black trumpets and their accompanying pan liquor make an exquisite complement for a good, tender beefsteak. Pour mushrooms and liquor over steak just as the steak is being served.

Also, because of the liquid produced upon cooking, black trumpets go well over rice. For that, refer to the recipe for shaggy mane mushrooms.

Grandma's generation had few or no field guides to mushrooms and had no way of telling that black trumpets were not poison. But today, we not only have field guides, but many are in color, even small beginner's guides such as this one. Along with the text, a good color photo comes as a considerable aid when identifying mushrooms.

Areas that host black trumpets remain productive for many years. However, this does not mean that the mushrooms will come up every year, because they don't. Sometimes, particularly during extreme climate events such as drought or too-frequent rainfall, black trumpets do not show at all. Also, while appearing some time in mid-August, the trumpets sometimes wait until later in the month or even until early September before appearing.

After picking black trumpets, make it a point to return to the same spot two or three days later, since these mushrooms don't all appear at once, and another flush of fungi may present itself in the same place that was already picked over.

CHANTERELLE
Cantharellus cibarius

Synonym: None known. Most everyone simply refers to this mushroom as "chanterelle."

Identification: Entire mushroom one single color, usually egg-yellow to a mild orange. Wide-set gills run halfway down the stalk. The cap has a waxy feel. Mature specimens exhibit a central depression.

Chanterelles grow singly—that is, while many mushrooms may grow in one small area, each one is a single plant. Chanterelle mushrooms do not grow in clumps, as in when stalks originate from a common point.

Because of their bright color, chanterelles are easily visible from a great distance.

Habitat: Chanterelles like softwood stands as well as mixed-growth woodlands. Chanterelles are mushrooms of the shade and never grow in the open. Chanterelles grow on the ground.

Use: Cooked mushroom, good alone and pairs well with other ingredients.

Similarity to toxic species: Jack–o-lantern, *Omphalotus illudens*, has closely set gills, grows in bunches at the base of trees, and glows green in the dark. Also, *Hygorphosis aurantia* can be mistaken for a chanterelle and is toxic to some people. It grows singly on wood and

Chanterelles, coral mushrooms, and pear-shaped puffballs

has thin, deep, knife-edge gills, unlike the very thick and shallow gill-like structures of the chanterelle.

Best time: Chanterelle is a summer mushroom and does best from July through August.

Status: Common and widespread.

Tools needed: Basket or cloth bag.

Storage: Chanterelles keep well in a refrigerator and will remain useable for two or three days. Chanterelles also retain their color and flavor when partially cooked and then frozen.

The Species

One day long ago, the author found a great many chanterelles growing in his mixed-growth forest woodlot. He picked a large basket full and photographed them, captioning them "Summer Mushrooms." But not knowing what the mushrooms were, they were discarded. Better safe than sorry.

Not long after, it became plain that these were very fine, safe, edible mushrooms. What a pity the first batch got discarded. But protocol demands we give all unidentified mushrooms the heave. Since that first encounter, chanterelles have continued to come up in the same part of the same woodlot, but never again in the numbers of that first time.

Chanterelles have such a singular appearance that they make an excellent choice to show first-time mushroom foragers. Like the gambler's ace-in-the-hole and the pool player's "bunny," chanterelles are easy to locate and identify. Just find the correct habitat, go out within days of a summer rain, and chanterelles should cooperate.

Some writers consider chanterelles one of the finest-tasting of all wild mushrooms. While they are indeed choice, the author has experienced times when chanterelles were so plentiful that he got tired of eating them. The same could probably be said for lobster, oysters, and any other fine food.

Other times, though, particularly during wet weather with frequent rains, human foragers must vie with garden slugs for first crack at freshly emerged chanterelles. Though called "garden" slugs, these mollusks are at home in the woods, too. And they love chanterelles. Not all slug damage is evident, either. Most times, slugs eat the caps, beginning at the edges. But sometimes they strike on the bottom of the cap, hidden from view. There's nothing worse than coming home, cleaning chanterelles and finding sticky, slimy slugs clinging to the bottom of an otherwise perfectly good mushroom.

During dry weather, slugs are not a problem. However, one thing remains for the forager to do, and that's to clean sticks, moss, and other debris from between the gills. Never attempt to wash off clinging debris, since wetting makes foreign matter stick to the mushroom like grim death. Instead, use a toothpick or point of a jackknife to lift out any clinging matter.

Because of their tendency to pick up dirt and other small bits of matter, it pays to make sure the collecting vehicle, whether bag or basket, is scrupulously clean before filling with chanterelles. Putting chanterelles in a dirty container almost guarantees that the gills will be clogged with unwanted matter.

RED CHANTERELLE
Cantharellus cinnabarinus

JIM MEUNINCK

Synonym: None.

Identification: More orange than red, the orange color is bright enough to be seen from afar. Cap on mature specimens develops depression on top. A network of wide-set, gill-like ridges on bottom of cap run part way down the stem. Grows to 2½ inches tall.

Habitat: On the ground in hardwood and mixed-growth forests, often in large groups.

Use: Cooked.

Range: Throughout Maine.

Similarity to toxic species: While differing in appearance, red chanterelle may be similar in color to poisonous Jack-o-lantern, *Omphalotus olearius*. Jack-o-lantern grows on or near old wood, while red chanterelle grows on the ground.

Best time: July through September.

Status: Relatively common.

Tools needed: Collecting basket, canvas bag.

Storage: Keeps in refrigerator for several days.

The Species

Red chanterelles can save the day if chanterelles, *Cantharellus cibarius,* are scarce. While not quite as tasty as *C. cibarius*, red chanterelles are edible and at the very least fulfill the desire to dine on fresh wild mushrooms.

> ## RECIPE
>
> ### Orange Side
>
> Available when garden produce peaks, red chanterelles make an interesting color contrast with green, leafy vegetables. Cut up mushrooms and fry in butter and serve with any vegetable that has contrasting colors. Swiss chard works well, as do beet greens and turnip greens.

5 Boletes

KING BOLETE
Boletus edulis

Three kings and a jester. JIM MEUNINCK

Synonym: Cep, porcini

Identification: Large mushroom, 3"–10" in diameter, to 8" tall, a bun-shaped mushroom with a moist, smooth surface (like a brown hamburger bun), sticky when wet. Color variable from biscuit brown, reddish brown, and paler; margins pale. Flesh is white and thick, becoming green and brown, becomes infested with worms, insects, and larvae with age, so always pick only the freshest specimens. Small white tubes with the tube (pore) ends appearing to be stuffed with pith, first white in color and turning yellow, olive, or olive-yellow as it ages. Stalk is thick and sturdy, becoming thicker toward the base. Often solitary and scattered and occasionally in groups of 2 or 3. King boletes do not change color when touched or pinched! Leaves an olive-brown spore print.

Habitat: In reverting burnt areas, along trailsides, and even around campsites. Often in shady areas near streams

Use: Cooked. *B. edulis* is considered one of the safest and choicest wild mushrooms to pick for the table. They are watery, so slice thin and sauté. Cook until crisp, perhaps with a strip or two of bacon. Eat or prepare as soon as possible; shelf life is short. Add to soups, pizza, and even barbecue.

Similarity to toxic species: Proper identification is critical as some boletes cause serious gastric distress. Also, king boletes can pick up toxic heavy metals, such as selenium and cadmium, when found growing downstream from mine runoff. Fortunately, Maine has few such locations.

Best time: Late summer into early fall.

Status: Not endangered or threatened, except by development. However, these choice mushrooms are locally abundant, meaning they are not universally widespread, but when found can number in good quantities.

Tools needed: Basket, cloth collecting bag.

Storage: Deteriorates quickly, so try to eat the same day as picked. Or, if that is not possible, cook and freeze. Also lends itself to drying when thinly sliced.

The Species

King boletes are a favorite wild mushroom and it's a banner day when they are found. Abundant when located, but not always easily located, thus making it even more dear when found. In addition to its culinary qualities, king boletes serve as a folk medicine in parts of Mexico. They are said to have antioxidant, antiviral, and antimicrobial properties.

RECIPE

Bolete Burgers for Two

2 king boletes
2 buns
¼ teaspoon soy sauce
¼ teaspoon balsamic vinegar
1 tablespoon butter
1 shallot, sliced
Pinch of garlic powder
Pinch of thyme
Pepper to taste

Cut a ½" thick slice of the white flesh. Slice off pores and tubes. Place this slice in a plastic bag with the soy sauce and balsamic vinegar. Shake the bag to thoroughly coat with the liquid, then sauté in butter with the sliced shallot. Sprinkle a pinch of garlic powder, a pinch of thyme, and pepper to taste, and build yourself a bolete burger. Cheese is optional.

PAINTED BOLETE
Suillus spraguei, also sometimes referred to as *Suillus pictus*

Identification: The cap and stalk are both deep red and furry, or scaly when young showing cracked gills. The bottom of the cap has pores rather than gills. The underside of the cap is yellow, making a nice contrast with the rest of the red mushroom. The flesh is yellow, too. The stem has a woolly ring, shown in the photo above.

Habitat: Painted bolete grows only under white pines.

Use: Freshly cooked or dried. A good mushroom to use to add flavor to other dishes.

Range: Throughout Maine, wherever white pine trees grow.

Similarity to toxic species: None, but several other boletes that grow under larch or tamarac trees have a similar appearance. These are not reported to be toxic, however. Still, when searching for painted boletes, pick only those that grow beneath or around white pines.

Best time: July through September.

Status: Common.

Tools needed: Collecting basket, canvas bag.

Storage: Will keep several days in the refrigerator.

Painted bolete caps

RECIPE

Painted boletes are easy to clean in that the soft, spongy matter on the bottom of the cap is easily removed. This is the material that holds the pores, also known as "tubes."

After removing the tubes, just cut the mushroom up into small pieces and cook in a frying pan the same as any mushroom. Painted boletes dry well. When dried and ground into a powder, a small pinch goes a long way toward flavoring mild-tasting dishes.

To pulverize dried boletes, just put in a blender. Don't add water. And when the boletes have turned to powder, stand an arm's length away before opening the blender, since fine powder can become airborne and the chances of inhaling it are high unless you stand away from the blender.

The Species

Some mushrooms stand out from the rest, and surely painted bolete stands among them. With its red, fuzzy cap and stem, these mushrooms can be seen from a great distance. The author has found painted boletes on his woodlot for many years but was convinced that they weren't edible solely due to their unique appearance. The good part of this was that it is best to assume every mushroom is at least somewhat toxic until proven safe. So the author was doing the wise thing. The bad news was that for years, perfectly fine, edible mushrooms went to waste.

The moral of this anecdote is that it is impossible to determine edibility or safety of any mushroom without going through all the steps of the identification process.

Many mushrooms return to the same area year after year, and so it was with painted boletes. Now in late summer and early fall, the author looks forward to picking painted boletes from his woodlot.

RED-CRACKED BOLETE
Boletus chrysenteron

Identification: Red-cracked bolete lives up to its name by virtue of cracks in its cap, showing red. Cap up to 3¼ inches in diameter, stalk up to 1½ inches long or slightly longer. Cap light brown in summer, turning darker brown in fall. Stem either mostly red or streaked with red. Tubes are pale yellow, turning blue where snails and garden slugs have nibbled. Flesh is yellow and slowly shows blue shades when cut or bruised. Leaves olive-colored spore print. This mushroom is a difficult one for beginners because some blue-staining boletes are toxic, causing at a minimum severe gastrointestinal distress in healthy people. *Exercise extreme caution with blue-staining boletes.*

Habitat: A mushroom of the woods. Prefers oak stands above all. Grows along country lanes and roads.

Use: Cooked.

Range: Throughout Maine.

Similarity to toxic species: Caution is urged with blue-staining bolete species.

Best time: August through October.

Status: Common.

Tools needed: Basket, cloth bag.

Storage: Will keep several days in refrigerator, but best when eaten fresh since flesh deteriorates faster than other mushrooms.

RECIPE

As with any bolete, it is necessary to remove the layer of tubes from the underside of the cap. This is easily accomplished with finger pressure. Then the tube-free flesh can be cut up into bite-sized pieces.

The best way, and the author's favorite, to enjoy red-cracked boletes is to slowly cook in butter in an iron skillet. The flesh might also be used in stir-fry recipes, and given the large quantity of flesh usually available when harvesting red-cracked boletes, it is sometimes wise to use in this manner, just to use up the mushroom before it begins to soften.

Red-cracked bolete mushrooms

The Species

Appearing earlier than most, red-cracked bolete kicks off the season for bolete mushrooms. This, along with chanterelles and black trumpets, gives the mushroom hunter a fair selection of summer mushrooms.

In addition to its early appearance, red-cracked boletes seldom show up as just one or two individuals but rather in fairly large numbers. Mature specimens stand next to smaller, newly erupted mushrooms. If these mushrooms appear a little small to harvest, try to resist the temptation to wait a few days longer because snails and garden slugs love to feast on the underside of the cap. For this reason, the mushroom hunter should not discriminate against small, immature specimens as long as their identity is absolutely certain.

Also, the stem often becomes tough and woody on older individuals, which gives us another reason for harvesting when young. This gives us whole, tender mushrooms, untainted by pests.

Note that when making a spore print, the image will show up in the form of dots.

Red-cracked boletes and painted boletes are just two of a large group of Maine mushrooms. After becoming acquainted with the boletes covered here, the collector may wish to learn about other edible boletes. But remember the mushroom forager's rule of thumb: Learn one mushroom at a time, inside and out. Then, and only then, is it safe to proceed to another.

6 Tooth Fungi

BEAR'S HEAD TOOTH
Hericium coralloides

Synonym: Coral hydnum, waterfall hydnum.

Identification: As with chicken of the woods mushroom, bear's head tooth is another easily identified mushroom, perfect for the beginner. The author's first impression upon seeing a bear's head tooth attached to a tree was that here was a large cluster of bright white icicles. And indeed, the mushroom's spines bear more than a little resemblance to icicles.

The whole mushroom is white, and with the pure white spines, or "icicles," hanging vertically down, the comparison to a clump of ice with icicles is a solid one.

Bear's head tooth mushroom may or may not have a short, stout stalk from which branches emerge and the spines hang down from these branches. As they age, they turn yellow and become bitter. There are two similar species, *H. Americanun* and *H. erinaceus.* Both are fine edibles.

The entire mushroom may grow to 8 inches or more in diameter, and the spines may reach a half inch or more.

Habitat: This strikingly beautiful mushroom grows on stumps, logs, and compromised or wounded hardwood trees.

Bear's head tooth mushroom JIM MEUNINCK

Bear's head tooth mushroom JIM MEUNINCK

Interior view of bear's head tooth

Use: Cooked.

Range: Throughout Maine.

Similarity to toxic species: None.

Best time: September and October. By November, the mushroom has begun to decompose.

Status: Common, where suitable habitat exists.

Tools needed: Collecting basket, canvas bag. Just break the mushroom away from the tree by hand. The spines are brittle, so use caution when placing in basket or bag.

Storage: Keeps well in refrigerator. Also freezes well. Not suitable for drying.

The Species

It seems that every dog—or in this case mushroom—must have its day. And once about 15 years ago, bear's head tooth mushrooms had theirs. It seemed that these mushrooms were everywhere. One golden October day stands out in the author's memory, with clear, blue skies, crisp temperatures, dazzling autumn leaves and bear's head mushrooms decorating the deep woods like ornaments on a Christmas tree.

A good number of bear's head mushrooms were removed from their trees and taken home. And that point friends suggested that these mushrooms, being

Fried Bear's Head Tooth Mushrooms

Adding cut-up bear's head tooth mushrooms to a variety of dishes always makes sense. These tasty mushrooms are sure to add a bit of flair to any homemade soup or stew. But just frying them, slowly, makes for the best dish of all.

In fact these mushrooms are so good when done to a turn in the frying pan that they work well as the main course for meat-free meals, either by design or happenstance.

So just slowly cook the cut-up mushrooms until they are tender. No need to brown them. Just pick, process, cook, and enjoy.

---

tough, were best used as an ingredient in soups and stews. But in cutting up the mushrooms, it didn't take long to realize that they weren't tough at all. So it was time to try the chopped mushroom cooked, to see if it could stand on its own merits.

The mushroom pieces, chopped and slowly fried in oil, were superb. Here was a choice mushroom, ready to be relegated to use as an addition to something else. Of course some bear's head mushrooms are tough, but the ones collected during that one glorious fall were as tender and as tasty as any mushroom going.

SPREADING HYDNUM
Dentinum repandum

Synonym: British people know this mushroom as hedgehog fungus. Mainers might follow suit, with a Maine twist, by calling it a "porcupine fungus."

Identification: Here's a relatively easy mushroom to identify. And best of all, it is one of the tastier mushrooms around. For starters, this is a cap-style mushroom, but the cap differs significantly from most cap-style mushrooms in that it has hundreds of little tender spines hanging down, stalactite style, from the underside. These cream-colored spines are soft and easily rubbed off. Also, the spines carry the spores, much as gills do on gill-type mushrooms.

The cap is irregularly shaped but with an overall rounded appearance and quite thick. The stalk is fairly short when compared to other cap-style mushrooms and has one characteristic that makes it stand out from the rest of the crowd: It attaches more toward the edge of the cap rather than in the center.

Finally, while some authorities list spreading hydnum as a brown mushroom, the top of the cap is anything but. The author likens the cap's color to that of an old childhood favorite treat, a Creamsicle. Creamsicles come in an orange-and-cream color, and that is just what

Spreading hydnum JIM MEUNINCK

the top of a spreading hydnum cap looks like. In fact, the author refers to these mushrooms as "Creamsicle mushrooms," a not altogether inappropriate nickname.

Habitat: Spreading hydnum grows in soil in both deciduous and coniferous woodlands. On the author's woodlot, these mushrooms grow where a red maple tree has almost entirely decomposed and gone back into the ground. Spreading hydnum can grow in small colonies of individual mushrooms, but sometimes a mushroom forager will find only one lone mushroom.

Use: Cooked

Range: Throughout Maine wherever its preferred habitat exists.

Similarity to toxic species: None known. Spreading hydnum, *Dentinum repandum*, closely resembles other related species, but these are edible, safe mushrooms too. Look-alikes may vary in color and size.

Best time: July through September.

Status: Common, but only where desirable habitat exists.

Tools needed: Basket or canvas bag.

Storage: Like all other mushrooms, best if eaten soon after picking. However, spreading hydnum keeps for several days in the refrigerator.

The Species

This is one mushroom to stay on the lookout for. Its thick flesh and slightly nutty flavor make it a real prize. Upon noting a location where spreading hydnum grows, make sure to check back each year, because these mushrooms return to the same place with a good degree of regularity.

It is interesting to note that in these cases where the mushrooms return each year, their presence has a lifespan the same as previous years. When they begin to run out, the returning mushrooms become fewer and smaller.

For the author and hopefully anyone else who becomes acquainted with spreading hydnum mushrooms, finding as few as three or four of the larger, mature mushrooms is the mark of a banner day.

RECIPE

Solo Side Dish

Like so many mushrooms, spreading hydnum lends itself to a number of cooking methods and can work in countless recipes that call for mushrooms. But of the myriad uses for this delicious mushroom, the best is also the simplest.

The author prefers spreading hydnum as a side dish. Being firm and dense, these mushrooms don't cook down as much as other, more fragile fungi. So cut the cap and stalk into bite-sized pieces and fry in butter or spread of your choice. Serve as a side dish along with any number of main dishes.

These fried spreading hydnums go well as a companion to many breakfast foods. Scrambled eggs, sausage, and a helping of fried spreading hydnum makes a hearty breakfast for any mushroom hunter.

---

7   Coral Fungi

Crown Coral, 100

CROWN CORAL
Artomyces pyxidata

JIM MEUNINCK

Synonym: None known.

Identification: Crown coral grows on rotting wood, willow and poplar in particular. The shape and points (typically 4) on the tips of the numerous branches are distinctive, crownlike—the entire plant is 2"–5" tall. Color is pallid to dull, cream, pale yellowish, tan to pale pink. Taste is peppery when raw (but remembering past admonitions, never eat any wild mushroom raw) and nondescript when cooked. Branches rise in from the fruiting body base. Flesh is white, texture firm to tough.

Habitat: On decaying wood throughout North America; widely available in late summer through fall.

Use: Cooked.

Range: Throughout Maine.

Similarity to toxic species: May be mistaken for gray coral mushrooms, which some authorities find of questionable safety.

Best time: Late summer and early fall.

Status: Fairly common.

Tools needed: Basket, cloth bag.

Storage: Keeps for several days in refrigerator. Not a candidate for drying.

RECIPE

No matter how crown corals are cooked, refrain from overeating, as that can lead to gastric distress.

Sautéed Corals

A simple preparation method is to sauté the mushroom in oil for a couple minutes, then add water, cover, and let simmer until tender.

Deep-fried Crown Corals

Crown corals are also good when prepared in a tempura batter. Coat cleaned crown corals with your favorite batter, then deep-fry in 375-degree peanut oil. Drain, add salt and pepper, and serve.

8 Hypocreales

LOBSTER MUSHROOM
Hypomyces lactifluorum

JIM MEUNINCK

Synonym: Lobsters.

Identification: Lobster mushroom is really a fungus that parasitizes other mushrooms, greatly changing their appearance. White forms of *Russula* and *Lactarius* mushrooms parasitized by lobster mushroom fungus exhibit a rough exterior colored red or red and orange by the fungus. The transformation renders the parasitized mushroom into something hardly resembling its original form. Easily mistaken for a mushroom that has gone bad. Harvest for the pot only those that are solid orange, the interior white. Do not consume any that show signs of mold or have dark red streaks, soft spots, or a brown interior. They are past prime and will taste past prime. All the same, lobster mushroom is beloved and eagerly sought by collectors.

Habitat: Woodlands, particularly mixed-growth woodlands.

Use: Cooked.

Similarity to toxic species: Since lobster mushroom is a parasitic fungus, it may parasitize toxic species. The transformation often leaves the species being parasitized so changed that identification becomes extremely difficult.

Best time: Late summer.

Status: Fairly common, but scattered.

Tools needed: Collecting basket.

Storage: Will keep for several days in refrigerator if stored in an open container to allow for air circulation.

The Species

Lobster mushroom was a virtual unknown to the author until one day while leading a foraging trip in Washington County, one of the participants hollered "lobster mushroom," left the trail, and came back with a rather ugly and misshapen, red-streaked mushroom in hand.

Several other participants gathered around to admire the newfound prize. These people had only recently attended a mushroom walk led by a professional mycologist. They explained that lobster mushrooms were choice, and it was a lucky day to find one. The finder took the mushroom home and presumably ate it that night.

The picture of that mushroom stuck in the author's mind, and upon returning home, he researched lobster mushrooms and learned their true nature. Several years later, the author located some lobster mushrooms of his own but declined to eat them because it was impossible to tell what kind of mushroom had been parasitized.

Lobster mushroom, emerging ISTOCK.COM

Fried Lobster Mushroom

People who have correctly identified the host mushroom and have eaten it as a lobster mushroom recommend the typical method of mushroom cookery—cutting the mushroom into bite-sized pieces and slowly cooking in a pan with butter.

Some adherents testify that this lobster-colored mushroom, in fact, tastes like lobster. Is this the power of suggestion? The only way to find out is to go out, identify a lobster mushroom and its host, and try some for yourself.

The chances of a lobster mushroom parasitizing a toxic species are small, and people have been eating them on their own for years without reports of toxicity. However, because the possibility does exist, people should not eat a lobster mushroom until affirming the identity of the host mushroom. Lobster mushrooms are included in this book of Maine mushrooms because they are fairly common and the host mushrooms are quite large. Several lobster mushrooms can provide many excellent mushroom meals.

Also, the effort expended in discerning the identity of the host mushroom amounts to time well spent, because it not only introduces the mushroom hunter to a number of other mushrooms, it also reinforces the step-by-step process involved in identifying new mushrooms.

Besides, it's nice to know the identity of common mushrooms, good and bad. Learning about lobster mushrooms makes for a positive mental exercise.

EQUIPMENT LIST

Items to take afield when mushroom hunting

☐ **Insect repellent.** No place in Maine is entirely free of biting insects. Some, such as ticks and mosquitoes, may harbor debilitating diseases.

☐ **Camera.** Even if you lack a way to carry a mushroom home, two or three close-up photos will help in identification.

☐ **Canvas bag or basket.** Use anything that allows for good air circulation. Plastic bags are a no-no because they cause heat buildup, thus destroying mushrooms placed in them.

☐ **Long-sleeve shirt and long pants.** These will help ward off infection from ticks and will act as a prophylactic against toxic virgin's bower and poison ivy. Long sleeves and long pants also keep mosquito bites to a minimum.

☐ **Field guide.** If possible, carry this and other field guides when searching for mushrooms.

☐ **Hand-held lens.** This can help in viewing gills and other important features.

☐ **Compass or GPS.** An old-fashioned compass isn't bound by battery life and, if used properly, can help a lost person find a way out of the woods. A GPS unit can mark the location of a stand of mushrooms so that the mushroom hunter can return with baskets and canvas bags.

☐ **Wax paper or brown paper sandwich bags.** These can be used to segregate unfamiliar mushrooms from familiar, edible ones in the collecting basket.

☐ **Trowel or other digging tool** for use in digging up the complete stem of cap-type mushrooms.

RESOURCES

Recommended Mushroom Books and Sites

National Audubon Society Field Guide to North American Mushrooms, 1981, Alfred A. Knopf, Inc. This guidebook covers all mushrooms found in Maine and features glossy images for each species. One problem, though, is that this 926-page authoritative guide is very difficult to navigate. For that reason, the book isn't recommended as a beginning guidebook but rather as a trusted resource for those hard-to-identify mushrooms.

Next, the *National Audubon Society Pocket Guide to Familiar Mushrooms* is a handy reference book featuring excellent, full-page glossy photos. This should be in every beginning mycologist's library. It also contains spore print tables for mushrooms cited in the book. A good companion to *Foraging Mushrooms Maine.*

In addition to mushroom books, some websites are devoted to mushrooms and these can come in handy, because they often include recipes and useful trivia. Here are a few:

- Taste of the Wild: www. Bio.brandeis.edu/fieldbio/Edible.Plants. This site from Brandeis University offers some solid mushrooming advice.

- 5 Easy-To-Identify Edible Mushrooms for the Beginning Mushroomer: www.wildfoodism.com.

- Field guide to common macrofungi in eastern United States—US Forest Service: www.fs.fed.us/nrs.pubs/gtr/gtr_nrs79.pdf. This site has fungi from all over the country, including some Maine mushrooms. Some good photos; text on each species; short but informative.

- Urban Mushrooms: How to identify Mushrooms and Where to Find Them: www.urbanmushrooms.com. This site caters to town dwellers, but includes some woodland mushrooms as well. Photos are quite clear and the text covers most of the important aspects of mushrooms cited.

Finally, the Maine Mycological Association offers lots of help for beginners and a chance to get together with other mushroom enthusiasts on field trips, lectures and other events. Contact www.mainelymushrooms.org/

INDEX

fairy ring mushroom, 32–34
meadow mushroom, 35–39
mica cap, 40–42
oyster mushroom, 43–46
shaggy mane, 47–49
yellow waxy cap, 50–52
glistening coprinus. *See* mica cap
 (*Coprinus micaceus*)
golden waxy cap. *See* yellow waxy cap
 (*Hygrocybe flavescens*)

H
hedgehog fungus. *See* spreading
 hydnum (*Dentinum repandum*)
hen of the woods (*Grifola frondosa*),
 64–67
 eating raw, 7–8
horn of plenty (*Craterellus
 cornucopioides*), 72–74
hypocreales. *See* lobster mushroom
 (*Hypomyces lactifluorum*)

I
inky cap mushroom (*Coprinus
 atramentarius*), 40

J
jack-o-lantern (*Omphalotus
 illudens*), 76
jack-o-lantern (*Omphalotus
 olearius*), 79
jewelweed (*Impatiens carpensis*), 7

K
king bolete (*Boletus edulis*), 82–83
king of medicinal mushrooms. *See*
 chaga (*Inonotus obliquus*)

L
lawyer's wig. *See* shaggy mane
 (*Coprinus comatus*)

lobster mushroom (*Hypomyces
 lactifluorum*), 104–6

M
meadow mushroom (*Agaricus
 campestris*), 35–39
 identifying, 3, 4
 spore print of, 5
mica cap (*Coprinus micaceus*), 40–42
mushroom of immortality. *See* chaga
 (*Inonotus obliquus*)
mushrooms, wild
 eating raw, 7–8
 harvesting of, 4, 10
 identifying, 1–3, 4–6
 locations for finding, 3–4
 preparation and storage of, 10–12
 on private land, 9–10
 species list, 15
 spore prints of, 5–6
 and "toadstools," 8
 and toxic look-alikes, 9
 See also specific species of
mycologists, 1–2

O
oyster mushroom (*Pleurotus
 ostreatus*), 43–46

P
painted bolete (*Boletinus pictus*),
 84–86
pasture puffball. *See* giant puffball
 (*Calvatia gigantea*)
pear-shaped puffball (*Lycoperdon
 pyriforme*), 27–29
pink bottom. *See* meadow mushroom
 (*Agaricus campestris*)
plants, toxic, 6–7
poison ivy (*Rhus radicans*), 6–7
polyporales, 53–69

W

waterfall hydnum. *See* bear's head tooth (*Hericium coralloides*)

wild clematis. *See* virgin's bower (*Clematis virginiana*)

Y

yellow waxy cap (*Hygrocybe flavescens*), 50–52

ABOUT THE AUTHOR

The versatile **Tom Seymour** is a professional naturalist and writer best known for his award-winning newspaper columns and magazine articles about the outdoors life. His videos and workshops have taught New Englanders about the joys of foraging for more than a decade. A native of Waldo, Maine, and expert angler, Tom is also a master of the bagpipes. His previous Falcon books include *Fishing Maine, Birding Maine, Nuts and Berries of New England*, and *Hiking Maine*.